# On
# EARTH
## as in
# HEAVEN

# On
# EARTH
# as in
# HEAVEN

*God's Kingdom, Power,*
*and Glory in the Here and Now*

# Geoff Daplyn

DESTINY IMAGE™ EUROPE srl
Via Maiella, 1
66020 San Giovanni Teatino (Ch) – Italy

*"Changing the World, One Book at a Time"*

This book and all other Evangelista Media™ and Destiny Image™ Europe books are available at Christian bookstores and distributors worldwide.


To order products, or for any other correspondence:

EVANGELISTA MEDIA™ srl
Via della Scafa 29/14
65033 Città Sant'Angelo – Italy
Tel. +39 085 4716623 • Fax: +39 085 9090113
Email: info@evangelistamedia.com
Or reach us on the Internet: www.evangelistamedia.com

ISBN 13: 978-88-96727-70-6
ISBN 13 EBOOK: 978-88-96727-84-3

*For Worldwide Distribution, Printed in Italy.*
1 2 3 4 5 6 / 15 14 13 12

# Acknowledgments

I have been influenced by many, many leaders and ministries over the years, and it is often difficult to remember exactly who said what. I have sought to acknowledge all ideas and quotes in this book. If there are elements of teaching I have used and not attributed correctly, that is my fault entirely.

But all those I have referenced throughout the book have been key influencers in my journey and I'm grateful to God for their ministries.

I'm also grateful for the support of the Your Kingdom Come team: Danny, Steve, Helen, and Julian.

# Endorsements

Probably the greatest need of the moment is for a generation to rise who are "natural" connectors of Heaven and earth. From the opening to the closing pages of this book, Geoff shares his conviction that a Kingdom (of Heaven)-minded people live above church politics or even church activity. They do not lower their expectations but live at a higher level, focused on the Father's presence and the glory of God changing the environment around them. Provoking but not condemning, challenging yet accessible, this book can be read to gain the big picture of our natural habitat and can also be read in bite-size pieces so that the presence of Heaven invades our core being. I recommend it because it will be a tool to help change mindsets and bring Heaven and earth closer, for and through us.

Martin Scott
Author, *Gaining Ground and Impacting the City*

A person could spend a lifetime reading Christian books. They are so diverse; but most of them do not change your life or even strengthen your faith. This book is simply different. First of all, a person of faith and wisdom writes it. Geoff Daplyn is not just a minister of wisdom and faith, he is a person who practices what he preaches. This book is a real encounter with our Lord who taught us the Lord's Prayer. It is a book that takes you into His Kingdom, His power, and His glory. This book is not about the theory of the theology of faith, it is about living in the supernatural. We pray about Thy will being done on earth as in Heaven. In other words, it is about bringing Heaven to earth. Do not just read it, enter into it and your life and faith will be changed forever. There are so many parts of this book that I would like to mention, but I will not. Read this book and you, too, will be involved in this journey from Heaven to earth.

The Reverend Canon Andrew White
Vicar of Baghdad
Director of the High Council of Religious Leaders in Iraq

# Contents

Foreword...............................................................11

Introduction.......................................................15

Chapter 1   Heaven and Earth.................................19

Chapter 2   How Heaven and Earth Work ...........35

Chapter 3   The Kingdom of Heaven....................47

Chapter 4   Between Heaven and Earth................59

Chapter 5   Heavenly and Earthly Life ................71

Chapter 6   Jesus and His Kingdom.....................83

Chapter 7   How Does His Kingdom Work? ........95

Chapter 8   The Presence of Heaven ................. 109

Chapter 9   The Power of Heaven ..................... 127

Chapter 10  The Glory of Heaven........................ 141

# Foreword

The post-reformation church has gone through a series of God-initiated movements, particularly in the past 100 years or so, each leaving a rich tapestry of heritage. Revivals, adult baptisms, spiritual gifts, healings and deliverance, changes in worship styles, learning how to express heavenly love and joy—to name but a few. Many of these movements have been simply restoring something that had been lost to the church.

Each of these moves has brought some level of debate—often passionate—together with gradual reassessment of long-held theological stances. None of these movements, however, have resulted in a final and definitive expression of church, although each has increased our understanding of God's Kingdom. Each has also had some value as stepping stones to help the collective church move forward, however unevenly and hesitantly.

Even with all this progress, there remains a very visible gap between the various expressions of church today and the Gospel that Jesus lived, together with the early apostles. In some ways, we could even go as far as to argue that the collective evangelical church has become everything that the apostle Paul struggled for it not to become: a church relying solely on persuasive words of wisdom, rather than demonstrations of the Spirit's power.

While it would be very easy to criticize, especially with the vantage point of hindsight, it is much harder to discern what God is calling us to move into, and give a practical biblical framework to allow that to be precipitated in us without ending in gross error.

In the writing of this book, Geoff Daplyn draws on his own rich heritage of spiritual experiences. That of growing up in the Welsh Valleys and hearing its testimonies of revival, of entire villages coming to faith, while other nearby villages were simply passed by; his involvement in the Brethren movement with its strong Bible-based foundations in which his own father was a leader; and his experience of the United Kingdom Charismatic movement of the 1970s and '80s.

I got to know Geoff during his time as an elder in an independent Charismatic evangelical church in Haslemere, Surrey, United Kingdom. During his eldership, he consistently released faith as he preached. He regularly prayed for people at the "Healing Hour." He also supported several evangelism and discipleship projects, as well as more practical community-focused projects such as debt counseling.

Geoff cultivated an environment for the prophetic to grow, seeing a number of people released into personal journeys of faith. Flowing out of this group came a rich vein of testimony of our encounters with God, often in unexpected places and unexpected ways. Since stepping down from this role, he has been leading small teams in ministry weekends. He has also attended various conferences, hearing contemporary prophetic voices outlining perspectives for the future church. He also helped me lead "Hungry" nights, where we set our hearts to seek more of the reality of God's Kingdom and a deeper intimacy with Him.

Much of this book is derived from the talks Geoff gave at our Hungry nights. He approaches the gap between what we have now and what Jesus lived through, exploring the last few words of the

Lord's prayer—Kingdom, power, and glory. He develops the idea of the Kingdom of God as a biblical and divine framework through which God's power and glory are expressed. Geoff explores what it is to be mature sons and daughters seated in the Kingdom as opposed to robotic servants or simply victims and perpetrators of The Fall.

Learning to allow God to challenge our perspectives on how we think He should work and yield afresh to His own unimaginable and often hidden ways, Geoff looks at the clash of the Kingdom of God with the enemy, seeing the battle lines drawn just as much within us, as without. Outlining some of the strategies the enemy has developed to disempower the believer, he sees discipleship being much more than a fresh adherence to a moral code or even a series of Bible studies, but rather reverently embracing the immediate presence of God and the supernatural.

Gatherings have to go beyond sermons, rotas, and performance to become places where we are demonstratively changed by the presence of God. We need to create space in our lives for God to be bigger than we have seen Him before, and to see this upside down paradoxical Kingdom as a place where the disowned, disqualified, disappointed, and disempowered are owned, qualified, appointed, and empowered to bring glory to the King of kings. Thus, we, as ordinary believers, are able to access the very resources of Heaven to release Kingdom transformation into our land in our "now."

Dr. Danny Webster
Your Kingdom Come

# Introduction

Sometime in 2009, I was preparing a message when I believe it was God who dropped a thought into my mind. It was really nothing to do with what I was preparing...and it wasn't in words. It was more a fully formed idea, a concept, a package, with lots of stuff in it. How can God somehow communicate so much in a single instance of time?

I spent some time unpacking it and struggling to get the words and the sense which expressed what I had received, and I think the bottom line was this. Father was saying:

> *I love meeting you in your world, in your ways, but increasingly I want you to encounter Me in My world and in My ways.*

Thinking about this and what it meant started me on a journey that resulted in presenting a series of conferences in the United Kingdom in 2010 and then writing this book. So what do I think God's statement to me means? Well, our world is the earth, the visible. Father meeting us in our ways probably refers to Him answering prayer to do with us in our world; protecting us, healing us, providing breakthroughs in relationships, finance, circumstances, families, jobs, and the like. Father loves to do all those things and indeed has promised to do these things if we put His Kingdom first.

I'm still working on what encountering Him in His world and in His ways means for me. But pursuing God on this journey has created in me an appetite to understand more about His world—the invisible, Heaven and the Kingdom that is manifested there. I certainly understand a bit more about that than I did when He first spoke it to me, but knowledge is still ahead of experience. Sometimes knowledge comes before experience, and at other times it's the other way around. God is not predictable, but He does have the last word.

One of the traps that those of us who are preachers and teachers fall into is being so passionate about what we are trying to communicate that we give the impression that *we* have the last word, the definitive explanation and interpretation of the Scriptures. It seems to me that we should be less emphatic and rather aim our teaching to extend to our hearers Father's invitation to journey with Him.

I trust I am not too emphatic in this book, and that you will want to join the journey. I have tried to include two elements that should be present in all good teaching, in my opinion: first, it must be a reminder of genuine biblical truth passed down the generations. This is good, but only a starting point. It provides doctrinal comfort and security, but can too easily be oriented toward the past. Those hearing only this kind of teaching week after week will not always be best prepared for what God is saying through the Scriptures for tomorrow. In fact, they are more likely to take a critical stance as they view the new things that God does.

Second, good biblical teaching, I believe, must also be revelatory. It may be referencing the same Scriptures, but it contains new insight from the Spirit that is future oriented, equipping for what God is doing and about to do. Martin Scott, a prophet originally from the United Kingdom, has said, "God gives revelation not information!"[1] It is God's truth that changes us from the inside—it quickens our spirits, and from that innermost part of us, moves into our minds, our emotions, and our bodies. It is revelation that leads to wholeness. It is how the Kingdom works, from the inside out, not from the outside in.

So, it's good to be able to say "Amen" to what we already know, but just as important to be open, perhaps even perplexed, at how the Holy Spirit can bring new insights out of Scriptures that might seem to have been wrung dry for years. This makes us dependent on Him again; and this, of course, is how it should be. He will show us what is to be accepted there and then, and what is to be held perhaps a bit more loosely.

So this book is aimed at those who call themselves evangelical Christians and provides challenges to current levels of faith within a biblical framework. What is old will be confirmatory, and what is new will hopefully serve to generate faith for moving into more of what God has for us. One of my favorite bands, Coldplay, has a line in one of their songs, "Give me real, don't give me fake." I have tried to do this as best I can.

Roger Bretherton says in his *God Lab* book, "In God's town, we are all tourists."[2] I have not yet experienced everything that this book outlines, but this is the direction I'm traveling. I invite you to join me, and welcome your feedback.

## ENDNOTES

1. Martin Scott: http://3generations.eu/blog; accessed December 12, 2011.

2. Roger Bretherton, *God Lab* (Eastbourne, Integrity Europe, 2011).

# CHAPTER 1

## Heaven and Earth

Have you ever heard someone comment about another that, "They are so heavenly minded, that they're of no earthly use"? It usually means that the person in question is something of a dreamer, with his or her head in the clouds and having little sense of the realities of this world. A sense of reality and how to work with earth's reality, the accuser would claim, is key to making any progress on planet Earth.

It would appear that many in the church, including church leaders, would agree. The number and size of practical activities and programs, both church and community, seem to have become one of the most important measures of success for "lively" churches. It looks good. An activity orientation within our church life seems to be essential for outreach and fulfilling the great commission. But is this really a Kingdom measure? Would it be something that would impress the King of the Kingdom, or should it be something different?

Reading the Scriptures, the "something different" does appear more likely to be true. In Colossians 3:1-3, Paul talks about having our *hearts and minds set on things above, where Christ is, not below*. If this means that we need a heavenly orientation about our living, rather than an earthly one, how does that equate with current evangelical and charismatic church life? It seems to imply to me that, controversially, the more we immerse ourselves in Heaven, the more use to the Kingdom we will be on earth.

In fact, Scripture declares that we are heavenly beings as well as earthly beings. Ruth Ward Heflin, in her book *Revival Glory,* says we need to stop looking to the temporal, *the earthly,* and start seeing the eternal, *the heavenly.* She prophesies that:

> there will be a time when we will be so consumed with the eternal realm *(of heaven)* that temporal things *(of earth)* will seem as nothing to us. So, we can no longer afford to live only in the natural realm.[1] (My emphasis.)

She isn't referring to the next life, but the current one. Paul says in Second Corinthians 2:15 we are to have this heavenly aroma about us, both for those who are being saved and toward those who are perishing. But isn't a heavenly aroma something that comes from Heaven? How does that come about? How can we develop and live in a Kingdom culture where this is the norm? And what does such a heavenly culture look like? How can we be aware of the invisible, and how can we be a lightning rod for the invisible to manifest in the visible?

God's presence emanates from Heaven, as does His Kingdom, His power, and His glory. All these elements have their source in Heaven, and God desires to see them all re-manifested on earth in a much fuller measure. We are called to demonstrate all of them in our generation. God's Kingdom, His power, and His glory used to be fully manifested on earth before the Fall. It was lost; but Jesus, through the cross, has regained everything that Adam lost.

How can we convert such doctrine into experience, into a normal Christian life? It seems inevitable that somehow we have to realign ourselves with Heaven if we want to make any real earthly impact. The kingdom of Heaven certainly seems to be an upside down kingdom as far as this world is concerned. So, as Michele Perry[2] from Iris Ministries explains, maybe we have also got to be upside down, with our roots in Heaven and our fruit on earth. Maybe we have to learn afresh to walk in two realms at once, the earthly realm and the heavenly realm.

These are the areas that we are going to explore in this book. If it was important enough for Jesus to teach His disciples about, then it's important enough for us. They were to be partners in this mission, to increasingly bring Heaven on earth—and so are we. At a recent conference, Rick Joyner said there is an incredible promise on our generation:

> There is a door standing open in Heaven, and there is an invitation for us to go through it. Those who answer this call will be caught up into the Spirit, with the result that they will always be seeing the One who sits on the throne. This is the ultimate purpose of all true prophetic revelation—seeing the glorious, risen Christ and the authority that He now has over all... never has the Lord been as personal and intimate with His people as He will be in these days. Believers will be in awe continually wondering each day what great new things they will see.[3]

So Heaven is open for business—and is open for you.

## INTRODUCING THE KINGDOM

So what is the Kingdom of Heaven all about? Both the Hebrew and Greek words for Kingdom have the central idea of God's rule and reign. So the Kingdom is about kingship, rule, and government. It is God's authority in evidence. Isaiah 9 speaks prophetically about

Jesus and His Kingdom, and says *of the increase of His government… there will be no end.*

So, under the anointing of the Spirit, Isaiah envisaged a time when the kingdom of Heaven would be manifested throughout the whole created order, in the seen and the unseen dimensions. Even now, wherever His rule and reign is acknowledged and gladly submitted to, that is where the Kingdom resides. It is manifested perfectly in Heaven among the angelic orders, who constantly worship God and do His bidding in Heaven and on earth.

However, it exists only imperfectly on earth at present, even among people who have submitted their lives to God, for not only are they saved—but they are also being saved. We know only too well that while our lives are dedicated to God and His Kingdom, not all we are and not all we do is legitimately Kingdom.

Where God's reign isn't acknowledged or submitted to, the Kingdom cannot be present. Therefore, that means that neither His power, His glory, nor His presence can be manifested. Maybe this is why signs of this heavenly kingdom are rarely in evidence either in many Christians or in many church communities. So, the crucial prerequisite for experiencing the power, the glory, and the presence of God is full acknowledgment and submission to His Kingdom rule.

Nowhere is such submission more displayed, in my opinion, than through John and Cath Butlin and their two little girls, three and five years of age at the time of this writing. They lived in the beautiful village of Christchurch in Dorset, in the United Kingdom. They described their life as "fairly idylic in our little middle class existence, near the beach in Southern England." But in their own words, they had become:

> …increasingly uncomfortable by the plight of the
> thousands of forgotten ones, that not only don't have
> a place to live, but don't have parents, shoes on their
> feet, or even clean water. We feel the pull of these little
> ones in our dreams and at the back of our minds,

underlying everything we do. An inner voice (often dulled by the clamour of Western life) is beckoning us to go out and seek those that are lost.

We're coming to realise that the Western philosophy of getting the biggest mortgage we can, the nicest car, comfiest sofa and prettiest curtains, falls far short of the responsibilities which Jesus Christ placed upon us. Even the lovely adage that our children (or grandchildren) come first as we selflessly work hard to do all we can to provide for them can often blot out the deeper and more costly path which our Father in heaven might have us walk.

He gave even His very son so that He could call others into His family. He paid the greatest price and made the ultimate sacrifice in allowing His Son to die so that we may have eternal and joyous life. He calls us to the same Calvary road, to possibly make the same sacrifices (that aren't really sacrifices at all compared to the surpassing joy that runs out of them). He calls to go lower, to stop for the nobodies, to make ourselves of no repute, to give up job and salary if necessary, to partake in His topsy turvy, upside down kingdom where those that have it all are at the bottom and those that have nothing are honoured like a royal bride to be.

He asks us in our global village not just to love our next door neighbour but to love the neighbour at the end of a twelve hour flight, pricking our dulled consciences with words such as "what ever you do for the very least (of these) you have done for Me." He challenges us to give up what we think is important and jump off our so important busy schedules in order to "waste our time" on the "unimportant." In so doing we find His heart and start to know our Heavenly Father deeper and so start to become more like Him; sacrifices become easier, it becomes harder to ignore His call in our lives and almost by accident we find a sense of His presence in our lives. We start becoming surrounded by, and indwelt by something far deeper and wider and larger than we could ever imagine, the love of God. Thank you for joining us on our journey....

Their journey led them to Mozambique to join Iris Ministries with Rolland and Heidi Baker. In their blogs,[4] they talk of the wobbles, the sinking feeling that they experienced as the time drew nearer to fly their young family out of the UK to Mozambique. In earthly terms, it made no financial sense, no family sense, or any other sense. Pessimistic and doubting thoughts piled in one after the other. Then the Spirit brought the Scripture to mind about laying up treasure. And they remembered it was to be in Heaven, not on earth! Here's a typical blog of Heaven breaking out on earth:

It's quite a amazing to think that 10 years ago the Macua people of this region were a Muslim unreached people group. Now there are over 6,000 churches, countless miraculous healings and over 100 people raised from the dead. I've seen some of these miracles with my own eyes. Last week at church a woman was wheeled in, in a makeshift wheel chair. After about 45 minutes of prayer, her feet straightened out, another half hour and one leg, which was shorter than the other, grew by about 8 inches in front of our eyes. Miraculous, but still a mystery and a spiritual battle. I've no idea why some miracles take a long time, some never, and some are instant. Every weekend a team trek out 4 or 5 hours to a local village.

Last week the team returned with many stories of healings after people were prayed for in the name of Jesus. A man with a swollen neck received prayer and his neck immediately returned to normal size. He fetched his deaf son; after praying 3 times, puss started seeping out of the boy's ear. A baby born blind with white eyes initially did not respond to prayer at all. The team was going to give up, but handed the baby to Heidi Baker, and then watched as white eyes turned brown.

Out here food has multiplied when there's not been enough. The lame are walking, the sick healed, the dead raised. Part of it is the desperation of the people. There's no national health service, sickness usually leads to death, and part of it is the faith both of the recipients and those praying. The people don't have all the Western baggage of unbelief and scepticism. They meet the supernatural daily. Every village has a witch doctor. Demonic visitations in the form of dark shapes, animals, or violent dreams occur nightly. No one needs convincing that the supernatural exists.

Then there is the faith of the prayers. Nearly everyone out here has made great sacrifices to be here. Many have chosen to die to their own desires and ambitions, reliance on money or prestige, they are warriors willing to risk all in order to see God's Kingdom come and His will be done on earth. That has involved being stoned and exposed to great persecution for some. I've found the greater the willingness to surrender myself to the Lord and lay aside my desires, the greater the sense of God's love, presence, and also joy. It's an upside down kingdom. I myself visit the local village here on outreach every Friday afternoon and will be going on my extended outreach, camping in the bush from Thursday evening from 15th July (2011). I really would appreciate your prayers.

This is no theoretical exercise. For John and Cath, this is not just for Christmas, it's for life! But they know about the kingdom of Heaven. They know that when the government of God manifests, darkness will give way. Everything about the kingdom is to do with the government and rule of God in and through us. We need, there-fore, to learn how to rule. John and Cath are learning. We can, be-cause as the head is, so shall the body be. The normal life of the sons and daughters of God must be about learning how to rule and reign on the earth, in the same way as the Father reigns in Heaven. We are to imitate Him. Those who overcome are the ones who will inherit, says John in his letters to the churches in Revelation. God's decree is as Jesus taught us to pray "on earth as it is in heaven" (Matt. 6:10).

How much we are able to learn to rule in the spirit, in a safe, comfortable, middle-class Western environment, is an important question.

## On Earth as in Heaven

So what does God in Heaven want to do on the earth? The an-swer to this question is key to understanding how He is going to bring in His Kingdom, where His power is going to be released, and what His glory will look like.

Ephesians 1:10 reveals what the Father's plan is. The relevant phrases: "to bring all things in heaven and earth together under one head, even Christ." When we get our minds around this truth, it's awesome. I believe there are many, many areas in Heaven. Jesus said in My Father's house are many rooms, many places (see John 14:2). Even now in the 21st century, we understand so little of what the Father has created in Heaven. Because He is an infinite God, can we even guess how big Heaven is?

But just think of the diversity in the visible creation on this plan-et. Recently, some Australian scientists have worked out that there are about 11 million species on earth, of which only 1.9 million are currently documented.[5] Whichever number you take, that's an awful lot of creativity. If that reflects our Father's creative nature in the vis-ible creation, perhaps we should expect there to be similar diversity, even a similar number of different creatures in the invisible creation. I don't know for sure, but it indicates something about Heaven that might give us a different perspective. Certainly throughout the

Scriptures we read about angels, seraphim, cherubim, living creatures, elders, the seven spirits of God, and a whole lot more.

This Ephesians text is saying that the Father wants to bring all these together with all the things on earth—the nations, the cultures, the peoples, the natural earth—and reintegrate them, reconnect them, under the lordship of Jesus. This is massive! And this is the plan that I believe God is working on right now. This is the direction in which history is going. This is what we are involved in. It's bigger than gifts, it's bigger than anointings, it's bigger than ministries, it's bigger than church. It's the earthly manifestation of the kingdom of Heaven!

It's as we see the big picture that we realize it's no small thing we're involved in. We are sons and daughters of the Father whose plan this is. He has redeemed us through Jesus and adopted us for this very reason. We have been raised up for the purpose of partnering with Him, in reconnecting and reintegrating Heaven and earth. This is our destiny and this is to be our inheritance! Jesus, in what we now call the Lord's Prayer, instructed us to command the Kingdom of God to come on earth. How's that to be? Exactly as it already is in Heaven. Nothing less. As it is in Heaven, so it will be everywhere else.

Let's first explore the extent that Heaven and earth are already linked. In the beginning, when God spoke the physical creation into being, His intention was that it should be a physical extension of His heavenly kingdom. We know that because He created the physical in His own image. Heaven is perfect, and earth was created to be perfect as well. So, He intended that His Kingdom rule should be perfectly manifested in the physical, as it was and is in the spiritual. To this extent then, He intended that the earth be an extension of Heaven, in that it should exist under His reign and according to His word.

There are many Scriptures that talk about *the God of heaven and earth*. Heaven in this context isn't the starry skies, but God's dwelling place, sometimes called the third heaven after Paul's experience. Heaven is His realm, His dimension. These Scriptures imply that He is God of the earth in the same way that He is God of Heaven. This came as a revelation to me. I had always thought that because of the Fall, somehow His rule on earth was somewhat less than His rule in Heaven. Totally not so.

Because we are so caught up with earth and the spiritual conflict on earth, we don't see things the way God sees them. It doesn't matter what satan does or doesn't do, God remains *the* uncreated, infinite God who has never changed and who will never change. He reigns in the same way the day *after* the Fall as He did the day *before* the Fall.

Also, because He is God of both in exactly the same way, it follows that there is an equivalence about earth and Heaven that I'd not appreciated before. Again, I had tended to think that Heaven was far superior to earth. But Jesus didn't die for anyone or anything in Heaven! And because God already had a creation called Heaven before He created earth, that creation must have in some way not fully expressed God's own being. So He created earth and then said, "Let Us make mankind in our Own image" (Gen. 1:26).

## EARTH IS NOT INFERIOR

Psalm 115:16 says, "The highest heavens belong to the LORD, but the earth He has given to mankind." So earth is vitally important to Heaven. It isn't second best or inferior. Earth is a complementary realm to Heaven, a relationship that cannot change. And so close was the linkage between Heaven and earth in the beginning, that the Scripture says God, who exists in the spiritual, came into the physical and communed with Adam in the cool of the day (see Gen. 3:8). Now think about this for a moment. It was God who came from Heaven to earth, from the spiritual to the physical. We never read about Adam having access to Heaven, into the spiritual, as we do now as born-again believers. Why? There was no need. He was already as close to God as he could be, for there already was Heaven on earth.

We don't know how long this perfect state lasted. Genesis doesn't draw a timeline for us. But one day it came to an end, and we call that episode, the Fall. However, Jesus came to reverse the impact of the Fall and recover everything that was lost by Adam. The atonement was and is utterly comprehensive. There is nothing that the shed blood of Jesus didn't achieve. Under the New Covenant, not only has God sent His Holy Spirit from Heaven to be with us on earth, but we from earth have access into Heaven, which is what prayer is about.

Jesus promised that where two or three are gathered, He would be present with them on earth by His Spirit. But Hebrews specifically teaches that we need to come into the throne room in Heaven, for that is the only place where we get help and grace to help in time of need.

We have already established that earth and Heaven are different realms. Could it be true that one reason why we see so little answered prayer is that we generally pray on earth into Heaven, rather than from our place of authority in Heaven, down to the earth? This is certainly possible because the veil has been torn. The barrier of sin that was forged between earth and Heaven, because of the Fall, was fully broken by Jesus on the cross, and we are now counted as in Christ. There is open access between earth and Heaven.

What we are in Heaven, will be what we are on earth. It doesn't matter so much what we do on earth, it is what we are in Heaven that will move things on earth. So many Christians and churches concentrate on what they do here—their programs, their initiatives, their outreaches—but what happens in Heaven determines the outcome of what happens on earth. And satan cannot touch what is in Heaven. So when we begin operating out of our position in Heaven, we change the atmosphere on the earth.

## FROM EARTH INTO HEAVEN

That's why prayer is so important—and even while I'm writing this, I understand why prayer is often just lip service. Most prayer meetings are so boring. We need to find a new word for prayer because it has become devoid of life and excitement. The very word has so many negative connotations. But if we could just see that this is an activity in which we enter Heaven, things would be so different. Hebrews 4:16 says clearly, "Let us then approach God's throne of grace with confidence." The more time we spend in Heaven, the more we can bring to the earth. As we confront the enemy, we should do it from Heaven down, not from earth up.

The role of worship is not just to invite God to come down to meet us, but to enable us to go up to meet God. Heaven is where our Kingdom identity is affirmed as to who we really are, the authority we have, and the resources that Heaven can bring to the earth. Ian Clayton, from New Zealand, has a powerful ministry and suggests that the earth is a living thing, which is why it groans, and that it is and will be our role to bring it back to the glory it had before the Fall—as we were the ones who gave away rule on the earth to the enemy in the beginning.

Thus, we are fully equipped to be able to bring Heaven to earth. It was one of Jesus' main commands of His disciples to pray that the Kingdom of God be, as it were, re-manifested on earth as in Heaven—to bring things about as they were at the beginning. This is God's primary intention for the planet, and always has been. He isn't going to destroy the planet. He's going to restore it. He is a transformer. He's in the restoration business. That's who He is. So, through the cross, Jesus has already restored the linkage between what's in Heaven and what's on earth, between what happens in Heaven and what happens on earth. Believers, therefore, have an open Heaven. This was foreshadowed by the incident with Jacob recorded in Genesis 28.

This narrative is essentially a revelation about the existence of an access, a portal, linking the kingdom in Heaven with planet Earth. On it, angels were ascending and descending. Now, "angels [are] ministering spirits," says Hebrews 1:14 and "sent to serve those who will inherit salvation"—that's us. Bill Johnson, senior pastor of Bethel Church in Redding, California, makes the point that God is revealing an open heaven over us through which angelic activity happens from Heaven to earth and back again, aimed at executing the will of God and bringing in His Kingdom.[6] These angels, it would appear, were going to and fro on assignment from God. In spite of the Fall and the sin and darkness that was loosed on the earth, God had no intention of retreating. He ensured that there was access from Heaven to the earth. Even if the angelic had to battle to keep the access open, for example, see Daniel 12, earth was to continue to receive input and direction from Heaven. We see evidence of this all through the Old Testament.

Jacob realized that he was in God's immediate presence and because of his positive response, he gets an amazing revelation. Although still with his feet firmly on earth, he says in Genesis 28:17, "This is none other than the house of God; this is the gate of heaven." But it wasn't and isn't just about geography. There was nothing special about that particular place. It was just where Jacob had come to on his journey. Wherever he had stopped, God had determined to meet him. It was all about Jacob's positive faith response to the immediate presence and glory of God.

I've no doubt that a negative response from Jacob would have resulted in an ordinary overnight stop, with no vision. Awesome though, we now know that this was merely a shadow of what was to come. The Old Covenant shadows were pointers to a New Covenant where their fulfillment would be experienced. The questions for us who are now under the New Covenant are: What is the Kingdom fulfillment? And how can we experience it?

## WHAT DOES THIS MEAN?

First, it is crucial that we align ourselves with Heaven and the kingdom of Heaven. I suggest that most of us are too much aligned with this world, its politics, its economics, and its culture. But how we think, what we do, and why we do it, all need to line up with how God sees things—and He sees things from a heavenly viewpoint. What may appear common sense from an earthly point of view may not be of the kingdom of Heaven. Remember Isaiah 55:8-9:

*"For My thoughts are not your thoughts, neither are your ways My ways," declares the LORD. "As the heavens are higher than the earth, so are My ways higher than your ways and My thoughts than your thoughts."*

What looks and sounds good on earth is not always the path God chooses. Prudence, safety first, and practicality may be our guiding principles, but they are not God's. His ways are often startling, always supernatural, and never predictable. Once we are aligned with the kingdom of Heaven, then we can begin to declare that transforming truth over everything we come across that is not aligned with God's Kingdom—and there's plenty of that. Whether it is sickness, poverty, abuse, intractable situations, or financial strangleholds, Father has declared His intention to bring it all into line with Heaven under the lordship of Christ. But how can we declare that with any power in the face of the kingdom of darkness if we are not aligned with Heaven and under His rule and authority?

Second, how do we get ourselves aligned? Romans 12 says we need new thinking—our minds need to be renewed, because naturally, they orientate toward earth and not Heaven. This issue has not taken Father by surprise. He has made provision for this. Every sovereign act Father does is an example for us to intentionally imitate. It's like an earthly father teaching his son or daughter how to play a game. He does it first and then says, "You do it like this." This was exactly how Jesus taught His disciples, "This is how you do it, now I give you authority to do the same…off you go."

The trouble is that we don't do it. When God answers our prayer and provides a breakthrough of some nature, we rejoice (that's good), we give the testimony (that's also good), but we rarely take the next step, which is to say, as a child of God, "If I watch and listen for what the Father is doing as Jesus did, I can do the same, in His name." Jesus said that He only did what He saw the Father doing. That's got to be true for us. So how can we do that?

Third, we spend time in the Father's presence. It doesn't matter what you call it—worship, prayer, soaking, carpet time, whatever—Father has already invited us into Heaven. Hebrews 4:16 is the invitation,

"Let us then approach God's throne of grace with confidence, so that we may receive mercy and find grace...." Where is the throne of grace? Heaven. How do you do it? By faith, as with everything else. If God grants you experiences as you persevere in this, then that's entirely of His grace. And there are many who have testified to some astounding heavenly experiences.

This may sound simple, but it isn't easy. Your flesh will revolt. Your mind will suddenly come alive with all sorts of things to do. Your body will suddenly become very sleepy. It is a simple test of how much your spirit is ruling your life, and how much your body, your mind, or your emotions are. As you set yourself to pursue this journey in these three areas, your life will inevitably become aligned with Heaven, your mind will become renewed, and you will have a heavenly aroma about you as you spend more and more time in His presence.

## ENDNOTES

1. Ruth Ward Heflin, *Revival Glory* (Hagerstown, MD: McDougal Publishing, 2000), 39-40.

2. Michele Perry: http://enochco.com; accessed December 3, 2011.

3. Rick Joyner: www.morningstarministries.org; accessed December 3, 2011.

4. John and Cath Butlin: http://life-is-more-than-a-salary.blogspot.com/; accessed December 12, 2011.

5. See http://www.guardian.co.uk/environment/2009/sep/29/number-of-living-species; accessed December 5, 2011.

6. Bill Johnson: www.bjm.org.

# CHAPTER 2

# How Heaven and Earth Work

So through Jacob, God signposted in the Old Covenant that there was a direct link between Heaven and earth. It was something that I'm sure Jacob didn't fully understand at the time. He would have been staggered to learn that this dream foreshadowed a complete fulfillment under the New Covenant (see Gen. 28:10-22). It shows that Heaven and earth were always designed to complement each other and work together. At Bethel, Jacob discovered that Heaven could be opened up to earth, and earth opened up by Heaven. The Kingdom of God was to be comprised of both Heaven and earth.

It might seem strange that earth, a fallen earth, has the capacity to impact a perfect Heaven, but that's what the Scripture clearly indicates. Matthew 16:19 demonstrates this linkage and goes even further. This is the passage where Jesus teaches His disciples about binding and loosing. Whatever we interpret this to mean, what is abundantly clear is that He wants Heaven and earth to have the same values. So, what is to be permitted on the earth is to be permitted in Heaven, and vice versa.

Jesus said to His disciples:

> *I will give you the keys of the kingdom of heaven; whatever
> you bind on earth will be bound in heaven, and whatever
> you loose on earth will be loosed in heaven.*

So here Jesus is both demonstrating the closeness of the linkage
that He wants there to be between earth and Heaven. In fact, they
must have the same values if both are to manifest God's Kingdom
and rule. This passage also indicates, crucially, who is responsible for
implementing Heaven's values on earth—*us!*

## EARTH IMPACTING HEAVEN

We are in a period when the kingdom of Heaven is here, but
also not yet. Heaven and earth are yet to be reconnected completely.
Nevertheless, Scripture teaches that earth is impacting Heaven all
the time. For example, when Adam sinned on earth, there was an
impact not only on earth, but in Heaven. Corruption entered the
earth, but the eternal Son of God in Heaven got an appointment
with death! Again, in Luke 15:10, Jesus says, "there is rejoicing in
the presence of the angels of God, over one sinner who repents."
A sinner repents on earth, and there is an immediate impact in
Heaven. We can legitimately infer also that when a sinner refuses
to repent, this too impacts Heaven. Notice the phrase Jesus uses.
He doesn't say that the angels rejoice, although maybe they do. He
says that there is rejoicing in the presence of the angels. So who is
doing the rejoicing? I suggest that all of Heaven has a view of earth
and is impacted by whatever reaction there is on earth to the truth
of the kingdom of Heaven. But crucially the Godhead is impacted
by repentance and rejoices.

Jesus said not even a sparrow falls to the ground without it having an impact in Heaven. Since the sparrow was considered to be the
most common and perhaps least valuable bird, Jesus is confirming
that every action on earth impacts Heaven. From the Old Testament
another example, Psalm 2:2-5 says:

*The kings of the earth take their stand and the rulers gather together against the LORD and against his Anointed One. Let us break their chains, they say, and throw off their fetters* [on earth]. *The One enthroned in heaven laughs; the Lord scoffs at them. Then he rebukes them in his anger and terrifies them in his wrath* [the impact in Heaven].[1]

What's this saying? Earthly rulers pass laws and encourage a culture on earth that is anti-God and His Kingdom, believing it to be reactionary and constraining (chains and fetters). This is true in our day. The response in Heaven is laughter, as God considers their naivety. He delivers rebuke and terror.

In the New Testament this time, Luke 2:14 says, "Glory to God in the highest [heaven], and on earth peace to those on whom His favor rests." This verse is directly about the birth of Jesus and the beginning of the kingdom of Heaven being manifested on earth. But it also reveals more about the linkage between Heaven and earth. Because Heaven and earth are eternally linked, glory given from earth to God who is in Heaven has in some way a direct relationship to peace from Heaven breaking out on earth.

So the Scriptures are clear. The truth is that whatever is done on earth has an impact in Heaven. Whether it is governmental policies, the created order, or human responses, all have an impact on Heaven. And the response in Heaven, in turn, impacts back on earth.

## HEAVEN IMPACTING EARTH

Spiritual truths are often signposted in the physical creation. It is part of the way God communicates with us. Paul, in Romans 1, says that the evidence of God's very existence is plain from the physical creation. We know that the physical heavens do have a significant impact on the physical earth. For example, the moon controls the oceans and their tides. The activity of the sun not only controls climatic events, but solar flares and sunspots cause great impacts on the earth in the area of communications. As in the physical, so in the spiritual.

It is Father's desire that His kingdom in Heaven increasingly impacts earth. While the impact of earth on Heaven is not always positive, the impact of Heaven on earth always is. The very creation demonstrates Heaven's potential impact on earth. It was created perfect. Yes it has fallen, but it still bears the image of its Creator. Throughout the Old Testament, God impacted life on earth with His Heaven in a whole variety of ways. Some impacts were miracles, some were visions, some were angelic appearances. But all were manifestations of the kingdom of Heaven on the earth. Although these were limited, and only done through His chosen leaders or prophets, God was nevertheless, flagging up for His people and for us that Heaven was still there and was still in charge of the earth. So at key points, the kingdom of Heaven breaks into earth to provide direction, resources, key victories, and the like.

As we flip through the Scriptures, here are a few examples of Heaven breaking in on earth resulting in what we call supernatural experiences:

- Abraham, in Genesis 18:2-12, actually meets with angels, and Sarah laughs at the prospect of getting pregnant at her advanced age. This wasn't a vision or a dream but an actual appearance in the physical realm.

- Jacob, in Genesis 32:24-28, wrestles with a man, or so he thinks, and gets a new name; "...you have struggled with God and with humans and have overcome." Jacob's hip socket was displaced, so this was definitely in the physical realm.

- Moses, in Exodus 3:2, encounters an angel out of a burning bush, and God then speaks to commission him for his destiny. Again, Scripture makes it clear that this was in the physical realm. It wasn't a dream or a vision. Moses had the opportunity to ignore it and move on, but he chose to turn aside.

- Joshua, in Joshua 5:13, sees a man with a drawn sword who turns out to be the commander of the army of the Lord. Again, it doesn't seem that this was a vision but an appearance in the physical. Joshua takes his shoes off, as did Moses previously, but we have no record of the conversation or even the reason for the appearance, except to encourage Joshua to continue to pursue God's way.

- Gideon, in Judges 6:12, sees an angel while he is threshing wheat in secret in a winepress. Again, all in the physical. The angel prophetically addresses him as *a mighty warrior*, which he wasn't at that time, but did become later. This angel turns out to be Jesus Himself.

- Samuel, in First Samuel 3:10, has a supernatural or heavenly experience. Here, the Lord directly calls him as a boy while he sleeps. This is not a vision or a dream, but a clear and audible voice in the physical. Although he did not know the Lord at this point, he pursues the voice and eventually gets the advice he needs to develop a relationship with the Lord.

- Elijah, in First Kings 18:38, has fire come down from Heaven to consume a sacrifice in front of an enemy army and their demonic masters, in answer to his prayer. Again, very physical.

- Elisha, in Second Kings 2:12, sees the supernatural chariots and horsemen of Israel as Elijah is taken up to Heaven directly.

- In Second Kings 6, Gehazi, Elisha's fearful servant, has his physical eyes opened and sees more supernatural horses and chariots in the surrounding hills, as Elisha asks the Lord to open his eyes.

- Isaiah, in Isaiah 6:1-13, sees the Lord and a company of seraphs (detailed descriptions of seraphs but not much of the Lord), who cleanse him prior to the Lord speaking to him and commissioning him. Interestingly, the Scripture doesn't say this was a vision, although I have always assumed it was. But was it in the physical? Did Isaiah physically ascend into Heaven in an out-of-body experience as Paul described in

Second Corinthians 12, or was it a vision with his body firmly on the earth?

- Ezekiel had a series of amazing visions, and at one point (see Ezek. 8:3) was physically lifted up in the air by his hair, and then God gave him visions. This was in front of the elders of Judah who were sitting in his house at the time!

All these incidents demonstrate God's desire for the kingdom of Heaven to direct and resource earth. It's good to remember that all Scripture is profitable (see 2 Tim. 3:16). If it's in the Book, it's kosher! So, if we believe that the Old Covenant, under which these things happened, was but a shadow of what was to come, then surely we can under the New Covenant, expect to experience the fullness of what the Old described. If the kingdom of Heaven is being manifested on earth in the physical under the Old Covenant, we have to ask the question, should we be expecting, and be open to, lots more such interventions from Heaven under the New Covenant? I believe so.

When we get to the New Testament writings, heavenly encounters certainly begin to pick up dramatically. Jesus began to manifest the kingdom of Heaven in everything He said and did. The stuff of Heaven was now happening daily. But there were four very significant points in Jesus' life, and there were three significant heavenly interruptions.

- His birth—Luke 2:8-9. Angels appear over Bethlehem, announcing good news of great joy. This was no corporate hysteria on the part of working-class shepherds. Neither does it seem to have been a shared vision. It is generally accepted that this was totally in the physical realm.

- His baptism—Luke 3:21-22. Again the heavens are opened and the Father speaks, endorsing Jesus as His Son. This was an event where lots of people were present, so it was not a dream or vision. It seems to have been very physical, although some (perhaps unbelievers) just heard it thunder.

- His transfiguration—Luke 9:28-36. Here Elijah and Moses appear with Jesus. Now we should remember that these men have been physically dead for centuries. But the Kingdom glory of God appears all over Jesus. The text in Luke says that they were discussing His departure that He was about to bring to fulfillment at Jerusalem. It seems clear that Peter and John were fully awake; for Peter, wanting to join in, makes his suggestion about building some booths. So this is a physical manifestation of Heaven on earth.

- The cross is the fourth event, but the heavens stayed shut! We know why. What did happen though, the veil in the temple between the Holy Place and the Holy of Holies was ripped apart. It signified that now the New Covenant had been signed in blood and no longer was the traffic between earth and Heaven to be very, very occasional. Now there was free access for the people of God to come into the very center of Heaven, the Father's throne room.

But not only did the Father want to release His people on earth to come into His heavenly presence, but He also wanted His Heaven to increasingly be manifested on earth. The tearing of the veil was not just to allow humankind to come into Heaven through the blood of Jesus, but to allow Heaven legal access to the earth again. It was to be two-way.

These heavenly encounters carried on at a steady pace in the early church. For example:

- Pentecost in Acts 2:1. Here the kingdom of Heaven manifests on earth as tongues of fire, a sound of a whirlwind, people speaking in other human languages they hadn't learned, and the 120 northerners getting filled with the Holy Spirit and appearing to be drunk! Interestingly, Psalm 104:4 speaks of angels as flames of fire and winds, so maybe this was an angelic manifestation.

- Stephen, in Acts 7:55, sees Heaven opened and the glory of God, with Jesus standing at the right hand of the Father. It is not clear from the text whether this was a vision or not. Neither does Scripture say if anyone else saw it or not, but the bystanders certainly believed Stephen saw it, because they were angry.

- Saul, in Acts 9:3, sees a blinding light from Heaven, and the voice of Jesus was physically heard. "The men traveling with Saul stood there speechless; they heard the sound but did not see anyone" (Acts 9:7).

- Peter, in Acts 12:7, gets an angelic visitation in prison and walks out with doors opening by themselves. "Peter followed him out of the prison, but he had no idea that what the angel was doing was really happening; he thought he was seeing a vision" (Acts 12:9). But clearly not! It was definitely in the physical.

- Paul, in Second Corinthians 12:1-4, talks about his access to Heaven. Just as Peter wasn't sure whether his experience was "in the body or not," so Paul expresses the same doubt twice in this text. Clearly, Paul's experience was so real that it was difficult to know which it was, even when he "returned" to earth. This is a significant passage studiously avoided by many. "Was it a vision, or did I really go there?" Clearly both were possible, he just didn't know which it was. But notice also that Paul talks about visions and revelations—plural. This clearly wasn't a one-off experience.

- John, in Revelation 1:10-18, had an amazing experience of the glorified Jesus, with a full description. Interestingly, the text doesn't actually say whether this was a vision, a trance, or he was actually seeing with his natural eyes. John had a series of revelations recorded in the book of the same name. Did he actually enter Heaven? Was he in the body or not?

Some hold that such heavenly interventions ceased at the point when the canon of Scripture was completed, as if there was no further need for such manifestations. Actually they didn't, but through unbelief and quenching the Spirit, what was meant for all believers, became limited to only a few people here and there.

Records show that people in more modern days, such as Mary Magdalen of Pazzi, Teresa of Avila, Bernardino Realino, Gerard Majella, and many more had such heavenly encounters. Teresa of Avila, commenting on her own experiences, said:

> In these raptures, the soul no longer seems to animate the body; its natural heat therefore is felt to diminish and it gradually gets cold, though with a feeling of very great joy and sweetness.[2]

Hildegard of Bingen (1098-1179) experienced ecstatic visions as well as revelatory and healing giftings. Thomas Aquinas seems to have experienced regular ecstasies. Francis of Assisi, as well as communicating with animals, was regularly lifted from the ground in ecstasy. Of course, these experiences happened before the Reformation and these individuals were Roman Catholic. Because of this, many evangelicals have tended to dismiss these records because of the many abuses in the Roman church throughout the centuries.

But in the Orthodox Church, there were also evidences of heavenly encounters. Seraphim of Sarov (1759-1833) was Russian and known for his transfiguration experiences. He was changed, while still in the body, into divine light.

Another unusual witness is Sadhu Sundar Singh, born in 1889. Converted when he was 14 by an open visitation of Jesus Himself, Sundar was shunned by his family. They poisoned his last meal and threw him out. He wandered the streets and blessed whoever took him in. His practice was to go into deep contemplation, and often he would be plunged into ecstasies, as many as ten a month. He said it was a gift, and he never sought it or tried to go into an ecstasy.[3]

Early reports of Methodist meetings in the United Kingdom, had similar characteristics. An early Methodist convert wrote in 1807, "I thought they were distracted, such fools I'd never seen. They'd stamp and clap and tremble, and wail and cry and scream." An earlier meeting was described as: "the assembly appeared to be all in confusion, and must seem to one at a little distance more like a drunken rabble than worshippers of God."[4]

John Crowder, in his book *The Ecstasy of Loving God,* chronicles all these and many more. He records that:

> Many of the early Desert Fathers, in the third and fourth centuries, experienced tremendous super-natural encounters, trances, visions and prophetic utterances, whilst also working signs and wonders. An eastern mystic, Simeon the New Theologian (949-1022) reported a "baptism in the Holy Spirit" that was distinct from the graces given to him through the sacraments, and which was accompanied by compunction, penitence, copious tears, and an intensified awareness of the Trinity as light dwelling within."[5]

Re-reading this evidence, it is clear to me that many godly men and women all through the centuries have had tremendous heavenly encounters as they determined to seek and pursue God in their lives. And it is in our generation that God is once again beginning to release His Heaven in such encounters on the earth.

After 9-11-2001, Billy Graham's daughter was interviewed on CNN and talked about Heaven. What she said provoked a lot of interest. Even in the church there seems to be a renewed interest in the things of Heaven and in experiences of Heaven. While many are suspicious of all experiences beyond their own, others are pushing in on the basis of the truth of Scripture. Heavenly encounters are great when they happen, but the basis of them is the Word of God—not the experiences themselves.

Many have become so embedded in the seen world, that they discount anything from the unseen world. Even as Christians, we have adopted the rationalist view of the world around us. In Second Corinthians 4, Paul talks of the unseen, the heavenly, as being superior to the seen, which is temporary. One day, this natural realm will disappear, but the kingdom of Heaven will never disappear—so focusing on Heaven is a wise thing to do. Patricia King believes that this time is a *kairos* time for these things.[6] There are two Greek words for time: *chronos,* which references the quantity of time, how much time; and *kairos,* which references the quality of time, what was the time about, its meaning, its nature. So what Patricia King is saying is that we are in a season in God where He wants to reveal more of Heaven and what this means for earth.

Zechariah 10:1 from the Common English Bible gives us a heavenly principle in this regard, "Ask the LORD for rain when it is time for the spring rain." This means that the time for getting involved is when God is doing it, not afterward—and the time for the Kingdom of Heaven is now! Are we going to dismiss it all, or can we believe for rain to see the Kingdom of Heaven impacting earth to restore the planet and fulfill Heaven's plan for the earth?

## ENDNOTES

1.  NIV 1984.

2.  *The Life of Saint Teresa of Avila by Herself* (New York: Penguin, 1988), 136.

3.  John Crowder, *The Ecstasy of Loving God* (Shippensburg, PA: Destiny Image Publishers, 2009), 184-185. Crowder also references a book by Janet Lynn Watson, *The Saffron Robe* (Hodder & Stoughton, 1975).

4.  Crowder, *The Ecstasy of Loving God,* 272. Crowder also references Joseph Ritson's book, *The Romance of Primitive Methodism.*

5.  Crowder, *The Ecstasy of Loving God,* 142.

6.  Patricia King: http://patriciakingministries.net and http://extremepropheticuk.org/; accessed December 6.

# CHAPTER 3

# The Kingdom of Heaven

So what is the kingdom of Heaven all about? In this chapter we can dig a bit deeper into it. We will need to touch on some aspects of theology and maybe a bit of church history here and there. Unless we understand what the kingdom of Heaven is and how it works, we will miss what God is doing in our day. The signs of the Kingdom, so crucial in evangelism, will not accompany us. And it is these, according to Mark 16:20, that demonstrate what is said, is true, "and the Lord worked with them and confirmed His word by the signs that accompanied it." Words without the works are merely pious statements, truth without power.

Traditionally, it has been assumed that the kingdom of Heaven and the Kingdom of God are interchangeable terms. Luke, writing to Gentiles, refers to the Kingdom of God, and Matthew writing to Jews, prefers the phrase the kingdom of Heaven to avoid the name of God, which was held in such reverence and awe, that it was not to pass human lips. While this might be true, I'm beginning to think that there may be another set of definitions that are just as biblical. We have established that Heaven and earth are different realms.

They exist separately and distinct from each other. God's Kingdom is perfectly manifested in Heaven, but not so on earth in this present age. So I will use the phrase the kingdom of Heaven to refer to the rulership of God over the realm of Heaven. Similarly, I will use the phrase the Kingdom of God to refer to the rulership and government of God over all creation, Heaven and earth, both the visible and the invisible.

Theologians of all persuasions have, over the centuries, offered a bewildering array of explanations as to what the Kingdom of God is. We won't go into all of these because they're not all relevant, and you may be reading forever! George E. Ladd, one of the foremost theologians of our day, has said in his book, *The Gospel of the Kingdom,* "There are few themes so prominent in the Bible which have received such radically divergent interpretations as that of the kingdom of God."[1] This slim volume is an excellent biblical exposition of the subject. One of the reasons for such divergence of opinions is that the issue is totally central to God's whole dealings with earth and His purposes for its future and destiny. It is a common tactic of the enemy to throw up a confusing array of viewpoints to mask the truth.

One of the most popularly held errant views that I've found among evangelical leaders and evangelicals in general is, that the Kingdom is any Christian work that is outside the church. For example, a Christian group at your place of work that is clearly not "church" in the traditional sense. Participants may come from any number of different churches or even none at all. So some say it becomes a Kingdom work, rather than a church work. Such a church-centered view, I believe, is not biblical and does not display the immensity that is the Kingdom of God.

## THE CHURCH AND THE KINGDOM

So let's tackle the crucial difference between the church and the Kingdom first. Psalm 145:13 says of God, "Your kingdom is an everlasting kingdom." Nowhere does the Scripture say that the church is everlasting. It didn't start until Pentecost and will finish when Jesus comes again. In fact, the church is merely an agent of the Kingdom in the period of time from Pentecost to the Second Coming. Whether we define the church as people, the Body of Christ, or an organization, it exists and we exist, to demonstrate and bring the Kingdom of God on earth as it is in Heaven. My definition of church is a group of believers working together to bring the kingdom of Heaven on earth. So, where an individual church, large or small, does not seek to serve the Kingdom of God, but simply to perpetuate and serve itself, it has ceased to be under the rule and government of the King. It has, therefore, stopped being an effective agent of His Kingdom. Yes, church life may still go on, and good work may appear to be done, but it will not be producing anything of lasting value for the Kingdom of God. Value in the Kingdom is not necessarily the same as value in the church.

Let me give you an analogy of a family business. The father is the CEO and responsible for the direction of the business. He has directed that in the future the business is going to concentrate on just selling clothes. But one son has found a good deal on shoes and he's buying them. A daughter is spending all her time finding customers who want hats, and she's actively looking for them. And the wife is doing something else. All seemingly good and profitable things for the family members to do—but not what the father said he wanted or the business needed.

Similarly, many churches are engaged in lots of good activity, but are not necessarily focusing on what the Father has directed. He has declared that He wants His Kingdom to be manifested on earth as in Heaven. It is His rulership, His government that is crucial—not what the budget says, not what the trustees say, not what the elders or deacons say, not what the founder or the president of the denomination says.

Our Father in Heaven is passionate about His Kingdom. This is why Jesus *didn't* say we should seek the church first. He said in Matthew 6:33 that we should "seek first His kingdom." It is also why he *didn't* say later in Matthew 16:18 *you* will build My church.

He clearly stated, *"I will build My church."* That's the deal: we seek the Kingdom, and as a consequence, Jesus is able to build His church. John Wimber has explained it this way, "The church is not the kingdom, but the community of the kingdom, whose role is to speak the words of the kingdom and do the works of the kingdom."[2]

## KINGDOM MEANS GOVERNMENT

Now for a little Hebrew and Greek. The Hebrew word for kingdom is *malkuth* and the Greek word is *basilea*. Both have this central idea of God's rule and reign. So the Kingdom of God is His kingship, rule, and authority in evidence. Wherever His rule and reign is acknowledged and gladly submitted to, that is where the Kingdom resides. Where His reign isn't acknowledged, the Kingdom cannot be present. Maybe that is why signs of the Kingdom are rarely in evidence in many places of worship. If the Kingdom is about the government and rule of God through us, it is important that we learn how to rule.

Isaiah 32:1-4 explains that as we take our rightful rulership place alongside the King, we as His children will release justice into the world and become a people of blessing.

> *See, a king will reign in righteousness and rulers will rule with justice. ...Then the eyes of those who see will no longer be closed, and the ears of those who hear will listen. The fearful heart will know and understand, and the stammering tongue will be fluent and clear.*

Christianity is, thus, about learning how to rule and reign in the same way as God does in Heaven. It is only those who overcome who will inherit. This is discipleship. This is what Jesus was teaching His disciples. He taught them to rule over sickness, over the demonic, over the flesh, over external criticism, etc. Discipleship is not a series of Bible studies!

Now the Scripture indicates that the Kingdom of God is both in the present and at some point in the future. It is now, and it is also not yet. These two ages are called *This Present Age* and *The Age to Come*. George E. Ladd has said that the Kingdom is the presence of the future! Simply, The Age to Come begins with the second coming of Christ, when the Kingdom of God will be completely and fully manifested on the earth as it was intended to be from the beginning. This Present Age, on the other hand, started at creation and will end when Jesus returns. In this period, there have been and are specific signs of the Kingdom by which we understand what God is up to.

We can see these signs throughout the Old Testament as God revealed Himself to His people, both directly and through the prophets. For example, in bringing the people of Israel out of Egypt, God demonstrated His rule over Pharaoh. The fire coming down on Mount Carmel in response to Elijah's faith, demonstrated again His rule and government over His enemies. These were signs and manifestations of God's Kingdom; and as we have seen, they accelerated enormously when Jesus began His ministry and continued through the years of the early church as the Holy Spirit was poured out. They were meant to continue throughout all succeeding generations. But over the centuries, we have been singularly unsuccessful in maintaining any measure of continuance and sustainability when God pours out His goodness in revival.

Much of this is because we haven't been taught who we really are, and what we have the authority to do. Human beings are spirit beings. When we are born again, our spirits are quickened, and we become part of a heavenly kingdom. We get adopted by God Himself. We came out of one kingdom, a pseudo-kingdom, the kingdom of darkness, which we entered by being born of water. We entered another, the kingdom of Heaven, by being born of the spirit. As soon as that happened we became kings in that new kingdom. Jesus is King of kings. As a king in the new kingdom, we are tasked to bring the resurrected life of the kingdom of Heaven, back into the earth in spite of the kingdom of darkness. God is looking for those who know they are kings. He wants to rest His government on them and enable them to rule. You have the capacity to rule. It's who you are.

In Matthew 8:20 Jesus said, "Foxes have dens and birds have nests, but the Son of Man has no place to lay His head." In Hebrew thinking, head doesn't always mean the physical skull. It can mean government. So I believe that Jesus was talking on two levels as He often did. What Jesus was really saying to His Hebrew audience was that foxes and birds have an area where they "rule," but that He had no place to position His government. But post-Pentecost, He has. We must be a people who say to Him, here is a place where Your government can rest—on us. Isaiah prophesied that the increase of His government will have no end (see Isa. 9:7), which isn't just going to be true in a time dimension, but also means there will be nothing that comes outside of His government. Nothing!

## THE KINGDOM INSIDE AND OUTSIDE

The kingdom of Heaven is both on the outside of us and on the inside. When the kingdom within has dominion over the individual, then the kingdom without can be clearly manifested. What is within, mandates what is without. We will not be able to see God's Kingdom manifested in the world and the people around us unless first it is clearly ruling within us. Jesus said that the Kingdom is within us. It starts from the inside and moves out, not the other way around. That means it is closer to me than the air I breathe. It is the Source of my life. So, we have the capacity to release the kingdom of Heaven into the arena of this world and to establish the dominion of that Kingdom over an earthly kingdom that is darkness.

The kingdom of Heaven exists both inside and outside time and space. These are specific dimensions in the physical creation which God has created for the earth. Earthly life on this planet is subjected to the dimensions of time and space. Heaven, on the other hand, was not created with these dimensions. It probably has dimensions of its own which we know nothing about. It is thus not subjected to time. Hebrews 13:8 declares that Jesus *is the same yesterday, today and forever,* because He is a heavenly being, albeit in an earthly body. So, yesterday continues to exist in the spirit. He is the God of yesterday. That's why and how He can redeem the past.

That's how He can forgive the sins of the past. The past is not a problem for God, for He is the God of the past.

Satan, although a spiritual being, has sought to make the earth his dwelling, and thus is captured in time and space. I believe that he cannot now exist outside these dimensions, so he cannot impact the past. He can impact the present and he can attempt to influence the course of the future, but he can only do it using human beings, as he did with Eve in the beginning. He can do nothing about the inexorable divine clock that counts down his time. When that time has come, he will be cast into the hellish inheritance that God has made exclusively for him and the demonic. We, as children of God, are part of Heaven's kingdom. We are heirs of it. Heaven is our inheritance. While we cannot change past events, we are, in God, able to change the impact of those events. This is what forgiveness is about.

God's Kingdom is all about living out of the future, today. Romans 4:17 explains how God operates and how we need to operate. He is the God who "calls into being things that were not." He sees what He wants the earth to be and calls it from the future into being in the now. As an example to us, David was a man who lived out of the future. In Psalm 51, he asks Father not to take away the Holy Spirit from him, when the Holy Spirit had yet to be poured out. In Acts 2:31, Peter says that David even foresaw the resurrection of Jesus.

## THE KINGDOM CONTESTED

So we understand that God has a Kingdom. He is a King, and He seeks to rule His Kingdom. From the Gospels we know that Jesus came to re-announce the Kingdom of God, and to proclaim God's right to rule the planet, all creation, everything He had made. Psalm 24:1 says, "The earth is the LORD's, and everything in it, the world, and all who live in it." That is utterly comprehensive.

Clearly, God's rule isn't fully manifested on the planet at this time. In fact, this right to rule is being contested. The truth is, that behind many physical entities lays a spiritual entity who is continually trying to control people, places, and things. Scripture calls him the god of this world. He has his own pseudo-kingdom with its own agenda, which is simply to resist God restoring the earth to its pre-Fall glory by re-manifesting His kingdom authority. These enemies want to retain the earth as their home, and they seek to steal, kill, and destroy what God has created in order to do that.

This is the background to what we now call the Lord's Prayer. Unfortunately, the translation of parts of this text from the Greek has been heavily influenced by the desire to turn these verses into a liturgy. For example, the sense of the Greek in "your kingdom come" isn't that of a request. The word come is the same word that the centurion uses when he explains to Jesus his earthly authority in that when he orders someone to come, they come (see Luke 7:8). This word come is a command, and it implies movement from one place to another in response to the command. A more accurate translation would be, "Kingdom, come from Heaven to earth!" In declaring and commanding this, we're using our grace status as children of God to do our Father's business, because this is what His will is. We are prophetically declaring that God will manifest His kingly rule and reign over everything that is His. We're declaring that enemies of His rule will be put to flight, and that God alone will be King on the earth, as He already is in Heaven!

So God in His invisible Kingdom creates a visible universe, and it's amazing. Out of all the universes, galaxies, planets, and stars, He creates a planet we call Earth. It is a planet with just the right set of environmental circumstances for the sort of life He wanted to create. This became an integral part of the creation where His Kingdom, His rule, could also be perfectly manifested on earth as in Heaven! So we read in Genesis 1 that after the process of creation, God looked and saw it was very good—all of it. But at some point before what we now term the Fall, something changed.

Genesis 2:8 says, "Now the Lord God had planted a garden in the east, in Eden; and there he put the man he had formed." So, within the whole creation, that was created "very good," God plants a specific garden in the east, in Eden, for man. Isn't it interesting that God doesn't yet let man go into the whole earth. We know that the Garden was perfect and was a place where Heaven and earth were connected, integrated. Genesis 3:8 says that, "God walked in the garden in the cool of the day." Isn't it interesting that they "heard" God walking in the Garden? So God's Kingdom, His rule, must have been in full evidence there. There was no darkness, no sin there, because those things cannot exist in God's presence.

But we also know that, at some point, lucifer had rebelled, and he and a third of the angels had been cast out of Heaven. Our knowledge is fairly scanty about this; but clearly they had come to earth—hence the appearance of satan in Genesis 3 and the subsequent Fall. He and his hordes, it seems, were already on the planet. So inside the Garden, God's Kingdom was fully manifested—but outside seems to have been a different matter. It was obviously already occupied by illegal squatters. Psalm 115:16 says, "The highest heavens belong to the LORD, but the earth He has given to mankind." So this was intended to be the area of humankind's domain, not satan's.

What was God going to do about it?

God's plan for humankind is stated in Genesis 1:28, "Be fruitful and increase in number; fill the earth and subdue it. Rule over the fish of the sea and the birds of the air and over every living creature that moves on the ground." He knew what was ahead. Satan's moves are never a surprise to the Father. If the earth was going to remain perfect as God had created it, why then the command to subdue it? Even though He knew things would go wrong, God still gave Adam and Eve the task of occupying the planet and taking their rightful position on the earth. God wanted the whole earth filled with human beings made in His image, from Adam and Eve who would bring it back under His authority and be wholly part of His Kingdom. In this way, succeeding generations of this family would gradually spread from the Garden to fill the whole earth and subdue it, overcoming and defeating the forces of darkness.

Once Adam and Eve fell into sin, that strategy couldn't happen straightforwardly. It meant that they had to be expelled from the

Garden and God's immediate presence. So, out went the rule of God and His Kingdom on earth, and in came the rule of the kingdom of darkness. In also came sin, sickness, disease, oppression, abuse, disempowerment, poverty, death, and all manifestations of the kingdom of darkness. God's rule and reign, His Kingdom, now became hidden in the physical, the visible, until God's plan of salvation, Jesus, appeared.

God could have destroyed satan and his hosts with a word. There's no doubt about that. But instead, He chose to defeat him through His delegated authority—humankind. Initially through Adam and Eve and their descendants, the Creation Covenant, then through Abraham, Isaac, Jacob, and the people of Israel, the Old Covenant. And finally, under the New Covenant, it is open to all those who choose to live in fellowship with God, submitting to His rule and reign—that's us—to partner with God in defeating the enemy.

You are the Father's delegated authority. There is no further plan. There is no Revised New Covenant!

So we need to recognize the enemy's objective, which was and is to ensure that the Kingdom of God would never be reestablished on the earth; that their rule would be permanent; that the visible, the material, would now be their secure home forever. That's why in deliverance, they are sometimes so hard to shift. They love to inhabit the physical. But Jesus came to restore the Father's Kingdom on earth. On the cross, He gained legal and total victory over satan to give us back the authority, the power, to start fulfilling the original mission. Which was? To fill the earth and subdue it, to have dominion. That's what it's about!

## AN EVERLASTING KINGDOM

God's Kingdom existed before creation. In fact, it has always existed. Heaven has been the place of God's rule and reign forever. Because our minds can only grasp things from when time began, we tend to think that everything started in Genesis. Not so. The Scriptures have quite a lot to say about before the foundation of the world. Genesis was only the beginning of the material, the visible, and of course time itself. So, in fact, there was creation before creation! The heavenly beings that we read about in the Scriptures were all created. The whole angelic realm was created by God—the seraphim, cherubim, archangels, warrior angels, worshiping angels, and many other of the beings described in Revelation, Ezekiel, Isaiah, and so on.

In Heaven, the Kingdom of God existed perfectly in the invisible realm. God's will was done completely. His Kingdom was fully manifested. But He had a desire to create a material dimension so there would be a visible extension to His invisible Kingdom. This time with a creation with whom He could fellowship and with whom He could have a voluntary, intimate relationship. A creation who would bear His image and be capable of willingly partnering in the rule of His Kingdom. The angelic was definitely not created for this, but this is precisely what man was created for—and this is why we have been redeemed. We were not to be a creation who would merely obey His commands, such as the angelic, but a creation who would share God's heart and inherit everything He had created.

God has never been short of servants who would obey His commands. He has myriads of them. A legion of them was available to Jesus if He would have requested them. That's not to denigrate them in any way, but the angelic were specifically created to be servants for the Godhead. As Hebrews 1:14 says, "Are not all angels ministering spirits sent to serve those who will inherit salvation?" That's us! They have been sent to serve us as His sons. We are not servants, for servants do not rule. The angelic are available to serve us. And God doesn't make provision where there is no need; so in environments where this truth is not recognized, it is unlikely that Christians will be discipled and positioned to rule and govern as they should. Maybe this is why many are weak and vulnerable to the enemy's attacks.

But because of the cross, the kingdom of Heaven can now begin to be restored to us and through us to the earth, as originally intended. Heaven can come to earth and be reestablished. Heaven and earth can again be connected, integrated, and together, which has been the Father's eternal plan from the beginning; as Ephesians 1:9-10 says, "He made known to us the mystery of His will according to His good pleasure, which He purposed in Christ, to be put into effect when the times reach their fulfillment—to bring unity to all things in heaven and on earth under Christ."

## ENDNOTES

1. George E, Ladd, *The Gospel of the Kingdom* (Grand Rapids, MI: Wm B. Eerdmans Publishing Co., 1990), 15.

2. John Wimber: Audio series "The Kingdom of God," released by Vineyard Resources.

CHAPTER 4

# Between Heaven and Earth

Matthew 16:19 tells us that God has positioned us, as His children, between earth and Heaven. We have the keys of His Kingdom, but there's a problem. These two worlds we straddle are almost complete opposites. It is very difficult for us to set our hearts and minds on things above as Paul urges us to do in Colossians 3:1. The physical, the material, the flesh is in our faces all the time. Earth's intention is always to demand our full attention, and it continually seeks to heavily impact us with its values and attitudes. Added to that, we come across sickness, depression, injustice, poverty, oppression, and disempowerment almost every day. We get used to it; and if we're not careful, we begin to accommodate it, come to terms with it, even accept it, which Jesus never did. This is earth, the world we live in—and yet Heaven has none of this.

Heaven's values are not the values of your employer, your political party, or maybe even your church! There is no sickness in Heaven, no disease, no depression, no lack of self-esteem, no weariness, no control—no religion in Heaven. And although we were born into this world and are physically living here, God declares in

Philippians 3:20 that in reality, we aren't citizens of earth anymore. He declares that our citizenship is in Heaven. Some say we have dual citizenship, but I find that the Scripture says otherwise. Jesus said His Kingdom was not of this world—and we are of His Kingdom. In Romans 12:1-2 we are urged not to be conformed to what happens on earth, but to be transformed. This is the only way that we can have Heaven's perspective.

It's as if we were living in a small fifth-floor walk-up in the Bronx in New York, but had a plush home in Manhattan. The danger is that we get so used to the Bronx, that we completely forget what we have in Manhattan. We are not to be so taken up with the world and its attitudes and values, that we are blinded to the resources that Heaven wants to pour out on earth. Heaven is there to resource earth. Wherever the presence of God is manifested on earth, there is a point of immediate interaction between Heaven and earth, a gateway, a portal. There is an opening for Heaven to pour out the resources that earth needs to begin that reintegration and reconnection—if we respond with the authority we have been given and use the keys given to us. As we respond, God's presence inhabits each answer to prayer, so that another situation, another person, another area is brought into His Kingdom and under His rule and reign—and a little bit more of earth is reintegrated and reconnected with Heaven.

As we have seen, the scary truth is that everything we do, or don't do, has an impact in Heaven. Heaven takes us very seriously; in fact, more seriously than we often take ourselves. After all, we are His sons and daughters, and this Father takes responsibility for His family seriously. God isn't like an earthly father who sometimes does, and often doesn't care for his family. Don't ever think you are forgotten, lost, abandoned, or orphaned. Heaven has a tracking system on you that knows where you are, what you're going through, what your desires are, and even more important, who you're going to be! Your job is to cooperate with Heaven and keep calling His future for you into being. Remember, God is one who calls things that are not (yet), as though they were, and He wants us to imitate Him—to do the same!

God wants to manifest His Heaven on the earth with increasing measure. He is going to do it through His people who, as they fellowship with the Spirit and spend time in the Spirit, are going to be transformed from one degree of glory to another. I believe we will increasingly hear of such things as visions, dreams, trances, revelations, angelic appearances—maybe in the body, maybe out of the body. This is going to challenge our Western rational and religious mindset. But God is going to be God. He isn't going to change. We had better get used to it instead of thinking God is going to do the seeker-sensitive thing on us. He isn't!

Rolland Baker's grandfather, H.A. Baker and his wife, ministered in southwest China in the early twentieth century. They ran an orphanage called the Adullam Rescue Mission aimed at providing a home for boys from 6 to 18 years of age. These boys had previously been street beggars, uneducated and undisciplined. Many were part of gangs who lived by the laws of the street. In the book, *Visions Beyond the Veil,* H.A. Baker records that as these boys received Jesus, the Holy Spirit began to give these boys extraordinary visions that challenged even the mindset of faithful Christian missionaries:

> In the Spirit, time after time, the Adullam children were caught up into this city (the New Jerusalem)—it was not a dream, but a reality. Their visits were so real to them, in fact, that they supposed their souls had actually left their bodies to go to heaven, or that in some unaccountable way they had gone there, body and soul, just as in daily life they might visit a distant place. Frequently when they were in Paradise and were enjoying some of the heavenly fruit that grew there, they picked some extra to tuck in their clothes to bring back to earth for 'Muh Si and Si Mu' (Pastor and Mrs Baker).
>
> They knew they were only on a visit to heaven and would soon return. Upon returning, when the Spirit lifted from them, they proceeded at once to search

their clothes for the delicious fruit they had brought back for us. When they could not find it, a look of great surprise, confusion and disappointment would come over their faces. They could not believe they had not bodily gone to heaven and come back with the fruit in their clothes. Walking on the streets of the New Jerusalem was just as real to them as walking on the streets of a Chinese city.[1]

Here are examples of many heavenly encounters in a real third world scenario. They go beyond Western rationalizing and are totally of God's grace. If as you're reading this there is an element of scepticism in your mind, then perhaps your mind needs renewing. Let's explore an analogy that might help.

## An Analogy

Imagine that you're a third world child with virtually nothing.

You are an orphan, maybe part of a street gang. You vaguely remember your mother, because she died of AIDS. You live in different places—wherever you can. Every day you go to the local rubbish dump to scavenge for whatever is there, maybe food to eat or something to sell. Most days you are hungry.

Then you are told that a famous Hollywood movie star is in town. There are thousands of orphaned and non-orphaned children in the city and the word gets around that this wealthy woman wants to adopt a child. You don't really know what that means, but it sounds good. Then she arrives in your neighborhood, stops to talk to you, and evidently likes you…a lot. Next you hear that she wants to adopt you—you, out of the thousands of others.

It's pure grace, undeserved and totally other. Yesterday you were in a pit—no prospects, no hope, no future. Today, you're out of the mire, feet on a rock, new family, new resources, part of a new world, and you're singing a song! Hallelujah! You have a future—though you're not quite sure what it means yet.

You want to be out of your world like yesterday, but this pretty woman explains that she can't take you out immediately. But she has adopted you. It's legal. You haven't met her husband yet, but she tells you that he has exactly the same feelings toward you that she has. He loves you, too!

Are you getting this analogy?

Your new mommy is a humanitarian, whatever that is, and she says that she is going to train you to do in your country what she does in other countries. Help people. Heal them if they're sick, cast out demons if they're oppressed by them, replace poverty with provision, take away bitterness, hopelessness and shame, bring justice where there's injustice, and spread the good news that people can have a hope and a future.

Yes, you're disappointed that you can't be immediately raptured out of where you are. "I'm a believer, get me out of here," seems very attractive. But there's clearly a job to do and she has promised lots of resources at your disposal. But, of course, you have no idea what world she comes from or lives in. You've never seen it. You occasionally see other Western people dressed smartly like her, and perhaps in some ways they're the same as she is. But these others go by in their cars and do nothing for you or anyone else. They are part of this different world and surely represent this different world, but they seem more concerned with their own lives, rather than looking out for people like you.

You hope to see a glimpse of her world, to interact with the things of that world, to see something of a place that is actually your real and legal home, much more than where you happen to be physically at this moment in time. After she leaves, she sends letters that you read over and over again because they are full of what this other world is like. It seems fantastic. There's no sickness there, no poverty, no crime, no exploitation. It's a place of peace, security, fulfillment, and contentment—so different from where you are right now.

She promises protection because she loves you. She says nothing will harm you. She says that you will be able to overcome everything that comes against you. And you begin to see your world through different eyes now. You see all that is broken and impoverished, and how it could change. You know some of the resources that you have at your disposal. You have the checkbook she has given you and how she's already signed every check. And your overwhelming desire is to impact some of the negative stuff around you, and transform situations through what you know is available from this other world.

But how will you cash the checks in a foreign bank? How can you draw the resources from there to where you are? Apparently, it doesn't just happen by itself. It's almost as if you need to go there and bring it back. But you can't do that physically. You fill in the checks and send them off and persistently keep following up. Sometimes it's as if the checks just don't get through. But you know the resources are there. You know your new mom is good and wants this stuff to happen. Because she changed your circumstances, you know she wants to change the circumstances of those around you, too.

Also, it seems that there's opposition a lot of the time. You can't quite believe that there are some who want poverty to remain, who deny that there is another world, who don't care about sickness and are content with saying, "There, there, everything will be fine." It seems that there are even some people from this other world, who although they say lots of good words, don't seem to make any impact whatsoever. In fact, some even say that there is nothing they can do. But you know the resources of that other world are easily able to do the job.

...and so I could go on.

Do you get it? We Christians are citizens of the first world who are living in a third world. We are citizens of Heaven, but live on earth. We are not to assume a third world mindset. We are not to be so taken up with the world, its attitudes, and values, that we are blinded to the resources that Heaven has—and that God wants to pour out on earth. Heaven is there to resource earth.

## GOD'S POSITIONING

God positioned David between earth and Heaven. He devoted a whole psalm to his desire for Heaven. On one level he is talking about the dwelling place of God on earth, the Tabernacle and the Temple. But on another, David is inspired by the Spirit to prophetically speak about the real dwelling place of God—Heaven. Psalm 84 starts with, "How lovely is Your dwelling place, LORD Almighty! My soul yearns, even faints, for the courts of the LORD." David says that even the birds of the air have a yearning to be close to the presence of Heaven. He goes on, "Even the sparrow has found a home, and the swallow a nest for herself, where she may have her young—a place near Your altar, LORD Almighty, my King and my God." This encourages him to set his heart on a pilgrimage from earth to Heaven.

The Scripture says all who set their faces this way are blessed. But not just them, even people and places they come into contact with are restored. Psalm 84:5-6 talks about the infamous desert place of Baca, or Baka, "Blessed are those whose strength is in You, whose hearts are set on pilgrimage. As they pass through the Valley of Baka, they make it a place of springs." Even third world places that are places of dryness and barrenness, get transformed into first world places of refreshing, restoration, and transformation as the blessed pass through.

But many people, good people, are living in Baca. Whole communities and churches are living in Baca. They have become so used to dryness, barrenness, and God not turning up, that when they get together, they have already made provision for it. If God doesn't turn up, then we'll do it ourselves! Sounds dangerously like an Israelite king who lost the anointing of God—Saul. It is true that sometimes we have to pass through Baca. But it is a place to *pass through,* not to set up camp. We only pass through when we know what is on the other side and that a place of dryness is not our inheritance.

For many, Heaven is just a concept, a biblical concept, a place that is a million miles away. Didn't Jesus say that the kingdom of Heaven was near? Lots of Christian people have no idea that we are to engage with Heaven. As far as they are concerned, it is just somewhere we go after we die. We get saved, live a decent, upright life, go to church, give our tithes, and love our neighbor as best we can—and Heaven is the reward. It becomes pie in the sky when you die.

Yes, Jesus said that in the Father's house there are many dwelling places; and yes, He did say that He was going to prepare a place for us. But He also instructed us to pray that Heaven would be manifested *on earth as in heaven.* That is in the now! If Jesus asked us to pray this way, it means that is what the Father wants to do. If the Father wants to do it, it will be done! If we don't pray and press in for it, He will find those who will. Increasingly, God seems to be calling Christians out of structures into places of hiddenness, where they will be equipped and empowered for what He is going to do.

David knew something of Baca, and didn't want to stay there. His confession is, "Better is one day in Your courts than a thousand elsewhere; I would rather be a doorkeeper in the house of my God than dwell in the tents of the wicked" (Ps. 84:10). He knows that the earth he dwells in is like Baca. It's dry and barren. He longs for Heaven and for the presence of the Lord. It was the continual cry of his heart throughout the whole of his life. In Psalm 91:9-11, he speaks from his own experience when he says, "If you say, 'The Lord is my refuge,' and you make the Most High your dwelling, no harm will overtake you, no disaster will come near your tent. For He will command His angels concerning you...."

Paul is another man who God positioned between Heaven and earth. Philippians 1 gives us some insight into his own longings for Heaven and the conflict between these different worlds:

> *If I am to go on living in the body, this will mean fruitful labour for me. Yet what shall I choose? I do not know! I am torn between the two: I desire to depart and be with Christ, which is better by far; but it is more necessary for you that I remain in the body (Philippians 1:22-24).*

Paul says that he had the choice, but that he had decided to remain in the body for the sake of the Philippians.

Ezekiel was a man who, in a vision, was lifted up between earth and Heaven. Is this biblical levitation? Ezekiel 8 records that while in his own house, in front of the elders of Judah:

> ...*the hand of the Sovereign LORD came upon me there. I looked, and I saw a figure like that of a man. From what appeared to be his waist down he was like fire, and from there up his appearance was as bright as glowing metal. He stretched out what looked like a hand and took me by the hair of my head. The Spirit lifted me up between earth and heaven and in visions of God he took me to Jerusalem...* (Ezekiel 8:1-3).

The church is meant to be a people who live between earth and Heaven, interacting with Heaven and manifesting it on earth. Moses went up a physical mountain, but he also entered a supernatural arena and received the Commandments and instructions for the Tabernacle for the earth. He engaged with Heaven. When he descended, the glory of God was all over him and he glowed so much he had to cover his face. Isaiah engaged with Heaven in his vision in Isaiah 6; and after he was cleansed by the burning coals, he received a commission to go into earth. Paul talks of his third heaven experience in Second Corinthians 12, although we don't get much detail.

The apostle John on Patmos engaged with Heaven via a series of visions:

> *After this I looked, and there before me was a door standing open in heaven. And the voice I had first heard speaking to me like a trumpet said, "Come up here, and I will show you what must take place after this." At once I was in the Spirit...* (Revelation 4:1-2).

When John came out of this engagement, he also got a commission— to write the Book of Revelation!

In all these instances, there was purpose. What was seen and heard in Heaven was for implementation on earth. Heaven is intent on resourcing earth. God has already positioned us in the heavenly places, not as a reward or to give us status. There is stuff to be done on earth. The trouble is that we continually try to operate from the third world, earth, instead of from the first world, Heaven, where God has positioned us.

Hebrews 4:16 encourages us to "approach God's throne of grace with confidence, so that we may receive mercy and find grace to help us in our time of need." Question: Where is the throne of grace? Answer: in Heaven. We can approach His throne simply by faith, on the basis of the Scripture. Whatever experiences God wants to give us as we submit ourselves to Him is up to Him.

In Jeremiah 23:16, God rebukes false prophets who "speak visions from their own minds, not from the mouth of the LORD." He asks in verse 18, "which of them has stood in the council of the LORD to see or to hear His word? Who has listened and heard His word?" True prophets spend time in the council of the Lord. Question: Where are the council rooms of the Lord? Answer: in Heaven.

God wants to position us between earth and Heaven so that Heaven's instructions, commissions, strategies, councils, books, etc. are released on the earth, and not just humankind's ideas and efforts. We are the conduit. We have the open heaven and God has positioned us as a broker of Heaven's realities. This, no less, is what we are involved in bringing about. If we don't get positioned, it doesn't happen. As we present ourselves before the throne of grace, He is able to reveal Heaven's answers and causes those answers to be manifested on the earth.

Revelation 8:3-5 shows how this happens:

> *Another angel, who had a golden censer, came and stood at the altar. He was given much incense to offer, with the prayers of all the saints, on the golden altar before the throne. The smoke of the incense, together with the prayers of the saints, went up before God from the angel's*

*hand. Then the angel took the censer, filled it with fire
from the altar, and hurled it on the earth; and there came
peals of thunder, rumblings, flashes of lightning and an
earthquake.*

Here's another example of the linkage between Heaven and earth.
The Book of Revelation can be difficult to interpret, but I believe
that this passage is saying that once we are before the throne of grace
and accept our positioning, the requests and intercessions we have
are presented to the Father, and an angel is tasked with hurling the
answer back to earth. Note the hurling. This angel is not jogging.
There is urgency in Heaven! The peals of thunder, rumblings, and
flashes of lightning that come from the throne indicate God's presence. These signs are not to be interpreted as signs of disaster; but
rather, the impact of the holy response of Heaven, hitting the corrupt
environment of earth and making a difference.

In the Old Testament, God spoke out of Heaven, acted out of
Heaven, saw from Heaven, and heard from Heaven. It implies that
Heaven is "out there somewhere," distant from us. To some extent in
those times, there was a distance, a barrier, between earth and Heav-
en. Because of sin, this was built into the consciousness of people.

But not now. New Testament realities mean that we cannot continue to cling to the same view. The veil has been torn. It no longer
exists. I've heard some say that the veil is really thin. No, it lies on
the floor in tatters. An old hymn has the line, "O rend the heavens
and come down," and some have adopted it as a prayer. But He has
rent the heavens, and He has already come down! I remember a
person in a prayer meeting, praying, "Just say the word, Lord, and
this person will be healed." The truth is that He has already said
the word! The New Testament says, "now is the day of salvation"
(2 Cor. 6:2). This verse is not the exclusive property of evangelists.
Salvation doesn't just mean being born again. It means wholeness,
shalom in spirit, soul, and body. As far as God is concerned, the
time for healing, deliverance, provision, transformation, restoration,
breakthroughs, etc., etc. is now! Heaven is increasingly manifesting
here on earth—now!

We have been given the authority. We have the keys. And God will inhabit each circumstance with His Heaven, so that another situation, another person, another area is brought into His Kingdom and placed under His rule and reign. And more of earth is reintegrated and reconnected with Heaven.

Are you hungry for this? Do you want to be part of God's move in this generation? Are you willing to use the keys of the Kingdom that you've been given? If not you, who?

## ENDNOTE

1.  H.A. Baker: *Visions Beyond the Veil* (Lancaster, UK: Sovereign World, 2000), 38-39.

# CHAPTER 5

# Heavenly and Earthly Life

Genesis 2 describes the creation of man and the type of life that God planted in him. Genesis 2:7 says, "Then the LORD God formed a man from the dust of the ground and breathed into his nostrils the breath of life, and the man became a living being." This man was Adam, and God breathed into Adam two kinds of life. First, He breathed in earthly life. That is, life to the human body; life that enables us to experience the world around us and to interact with other human beings. So Adam's heart began to pump, his brain and nervous system began to work, and his will and emotions began to function. Also, God created within him, and subsequently Eve, the ability and the authority to reproduce this earthly life.

But God also breathed into Adam heavenly life. By this, I mean life from the kingdom of Heaven, a spirit life. This is sometimes translated in Scripture as eternal life, but the problem with that translation, is that it emphasizes more the length of life, rather than its origins and its quality. If you remember, the animal kingdom had their earthly life given to them by the command of God. *Let there be…and it was so.* But with Adam, God breathed into him, almost mouth to mouth, and the Hebrew word here for breathe is *pneuma,* which means spirit.

It was this heavenly life that enabled Adam to live together in harmony with God. It was God's own life, divine life. Heaven and earth were harmonious and integrated under God's rule. This was how creation was meant to be. So Adam received the fullness of life, which God breathed into him, and daily he lived in the good of it. God's Kingdom was fully evident as He came into the Garden where Adam was, and communed with him in the cool of the day. There were no barriers. Earthly life and heavenly life coexisted within Adam. This was how human beings were meant to live.

The Fall, however, meant that the heavenly life of Adam and Eve was cut off, although they both continued to experience earthly life. But now, even this was marred. In the absence of God's heavenly life, earthly life became adulterated with sickness, disease, and death as the kingdom of darkness began to extract its wages from humankind. The earth was made by God for man, but man had just given the keys away to satan for nothing.

## ACCESSING HEAVENLY LIFE

What do the Scriptures say about this heavenly life? In Second Corinthians 3:6, Paul talks about how "the letter kills, but the Spirit gives life." Certainly a well-known Scripture, but what life is Paul talking about when he says the Spirit gives life? Although the Spirit can and does give physical life, that is not what he's talking about here. He's talking about heavenly life that God gives through His Spirit, which is accessible to those who have the Spirit of God dwelling in them.

In Colossians 3:3, Paul says, "your life is now hidden with Christ in God." Again, Paul isn't talking about earthly life. Our earthly life is here. He's talking about heavenly life. In John 7:38, Jesus said on the last day of the feast, "Whoever believes in Me, as Scripture has said, streams of living water will flow from within them." This living water is referring to something supernatural, something from Heaven, not from earth. The same in John 4:14 where Jesus says to the woman at the well, "Whoever drinks the water I give him will never thirst. Indeed, the water I give him will become in him a spring of water welling up to eternal life."

The Spirit indwells us precisely to enable us to access Heaven's life. He is not there to give us a better earthly life, but to impart heavenly life to us. Peter said to Jesus in John 6:68, "to whom shall we go? You have the words of eternal [heavenly] life." He wasn't talking about earthly life. Listen to what Paul says to Timothy in First Timothy 6:12, "take hold of the eternal life [the heavenly life] to which you were called." Paul is not urging Timothy to go out a little more, get some hobbies, do some traveling, live life to the full. He's not talking about Timothy's earthly life at all. He's talking about Timothy's heavenly life. He's saying, Timothy, you have not only been given earthly life, but also heavenly life. Don't just passively accept it as a doctrine. Take hold of it, access it, be a man who actively uses it. Bring it to bear on your earthly life and the circumstances around you.

There are many people on this planet who believe that this earthly life is all there is. They know nothing of a transcendent heavenly life. But each person who has the Holy Spirit indwelling them knows that because they repented of their sin and surrendered their lives to Jesus, heavenly life has been restored to them. It is a love gift from God. How? Because of Jesus. The cross has restored to us everything that Adam lost. The veil of the temple, which symbolized the barrier between Heaven and earth, between us and God, was ripped apart. God, by His Holy Spirit, now has free access to the earth, and we have free access into Heaven.

Let me ask you a provocative question: If the Spirit's presence on earth is real and sometimes with physical impact, how real and physical is our entry into Heaven supposed to be?

## Heavenly Life Is God's Life

Second Peter 1:4 says we are "partakers of the divine nature" (NASB). God has breathed into us, breathed into you, a new heavenly life—His life. We have been born anew. Just as the Spirit overshadowed Mary and Heaven's DNA was imparted to her, so when we are born again, Heaven's DNA is imparted to us. God's own life. We actually share His life. That heavenly life that the Spirit of God is imparting to you is a portion of God's own life dwelling in you. We are supposed to live on earth out of that heavenly life that Jesus recovered for us.

I wonder why many Christians are still living purely out of their earthly life. Encounters with God have become either book-based, meeting-based, or both. Don't misunderstand me, the book is great; and meetings are a good idea (neither of which Adam had, of course. He just communed with God in the cool of the day!). But God never intended that His encounters with His children should be limited in any way. He is God Unlimited. Maybe we have cut ourselves off from more intimate and personal encounters with God. There has been a tendency in evangelical circles over the years, to minimize the emotional. It has led some to dismiss subjective experiences, feelings, etc., which might lead people astray into false doctrine. However, trying to safeguard ourselves from doctrinal error and defending ourselves from emotional hype, seems to have prevented us from being open to intimate communion with the Father, as Adam had.

But instinctively, we know that there is more. Both more than we have already experienced, and more than just our earthly life has the power to give. We have had heavenly life restored to us through Jesus, which is meant to enable us to encounter the Father. If encountering God and His heavenly life is important, when did you last encounter God and experience His heavenly life? I don't mean, when did you last have a sense of God's presence in a meeting? I mean, when did you last encounter God? And when did you last take hold of that heavenly life you have and release it into a situation, on a person in need, in order to bring it or the person into line with the kingdom of Heaven?

Are you hungry for that? Or are you content living your earthly life, unaware that there is a heavenly life that you have access into?

Each believer represents the kingdom of Heaven in this world. We are ambassadors. Our houses are embassies. We are to bring a manifestation of Heaven into this world. You are a citizen of Heaven, says Paul in Philippians 3:20. As Martin Scott explains:

> Read through non-Hebrew oriented eyes we will probably understand Paul to be meaning that 'this world is not our home and we are just passing through,' when he uses 'our citizenship is in heaven.' But read through Hebrew-eyes and having some understanding of the cultural background pushes us in another direction all-together.
>
> Rome was heavily populated and there was no desire to bring more people to the capital. There were pressures on the infrastructure of the city, so there was a policy of planting colonies of Rome throughout the Empire in other cities. If one was born free in those cities, the people would be citizens of Rome. Philippi (a Greek city) was one such city. The calling of those who lived in those cities was to live under the customs and patterns of Rome, and to make their city just like Rome. Paul is effectively saying, 'You were born free, live your life guided by heaven's patterns, make Philippi on earth similar to God's heaven above.'
>
> When life was hostile in these cities, the Roman citizens were not to ask to be taken to Rome for an easier life, rather they were to ask for help from Rome, and one day they would be privileged to have the Emperor himself visit. Indeed they might need the visit of the Emperor to enforce Rome's values in a given city. That visit would be known as a *parousia*, the common New Testament term for what we call the return of Jesus.

Now when we read the Scripture through those eyes, we see it is not about life in heaven, but heaven's life on earth now, and at his appearance a total transformation taking place.[1]

Heaven is our standard. It is where God's Kingdom is fully and perfectly manifested. Earth is to be transformed into an image of Heaven. We have been given heavenly life in order to establish it on a fallen earth, wherever we can. In this way, a fallen order is restored and brought into line with the standard—Heaven. *Your kingdom come, Your will be done, on earth as in heaven.* Earth, if you like, is a colony of Heaven, and God has made us partners with Him in bringing it back into line, in the name of Jesus.

That's what heavenly life is for.

And Jesus lived His heavenly life fully, while living His earthly life fully. He demonstrated what Hebrews 6 says when it talks about the powers of the age to come breaking into this present age. In other words, your heavenly life should be breaking in, breaking over, breaking through your earthly life, and the earth culture and norms around you.

## HEAVENLY LIFE IS COSTLY

What does this all mean? First, it means that you are not just another Christian, among thousands of other Christians. You have God's very life within you. This heavenly life, which the Spirit of God has breathed into you, is very precious. God is very jealous of His life. As human beings, we are not just insignificant beings who live insignificant lives, and hope that someday we'll go to Heaven. We're much more important than that. We are the crown of God's creation. We are joint heirs with Christ; and as Hebrews 1:5 says, "to which of the angels did God ever say, 'You are My Son; today I have become your Father?' Or again, 'I will be his Father, and he will be my Son'"? You are now a son or daughter of God, made in His image, to do what He does.

If you really believe that you are to be like Him, your life will begin to change. Jesus said He was to be the firstborn of many—you are one of the many!

God deliberately gave human beings the ability and authority to reproduce earthly life. When God took the female out of Adam, for the first time God created male and female as separate beings, who now had the ability to procreate after their kind. But He did not give humankind any ability or authority to reproduce heavenly life. Our parents gave us earthly life, but God has given us heavenly life. You will remember that once man had sinned, the tree of life was guarded, and man was put out of the Garden. Only God has the ability and authority to impart His heavenly life—and He doesn't do it randomly. Heavenly life for each of us cost Jesus His own earthly life—it's sacred.

The Father is going to look after it, which means He's going to look after you. You didn't receive heavenly life by accident. He loved you and worked to bring you to a place where you could receive it. So the fact that you have His heavenly life signifies that God loves you very much and will always look after you. In Second Corinthians 4:7, Paul says we have a treasure [God's heavenly life] in jars of clay [our human bodies]. It's a treasure. Having received this heavenly life, you are now able to commune with God as Adam did. In fact, better than Adam. He never had the Holy Spirit dwelling within him—you do. Jesus is called the last Adam. First Corinthians 15:45 says, "The first man Adam became a living being; the last Adam, Jesus, a life-giving spirit."

What does this mean? Remember, Adam, who was created as a living being, lost his heavenly life when he sinned. Ever since then, only Adam's earthly life has been passed to everyone. The Scripture says that we are spiritually dead. In the natural, there is no heavenly life in us.

However, Jesus brought an end to that, because He became a life-giving Spirit, who had the power and authority to re-impart divine, heavenly life to all who would accept Him. We can now live with both earthly and heavenly life within us. We can again commune with the Father, commune with Jesus, commune with the Spirit— as we were created to do. Our old natures have been crucified. That doesn't mean we don't have the ability to sin, because patently we do, and we're still Christians. But it means we can't anymore blame it on the old nature, the old instincts, the old urges. We now have full and total responsibility.

We can come into His presence, find grace to help in time of need, find strength when we're weak, find inspiration when we're dry, find motivation when we've almost given up. Yes, there are things that would try to block our intimacy with God. Our own flesh wars against the Spirit. We also have an enemy who is constantly looking for ways to steal what God has given us. These challenges are to be overcome. The tree of life is accessible to you again. You can eat as much of it as you're hungry for.

In Colossians 3:2, Paul urges the Colossian church to set their minds and hearts on things above where Christ is, not on earthly things. Everywhere lives are busy and pressured, with lots of work to do. There are many places where your heart and mind might be set. You may have friends or work colleagues who are not Christians. Where are their hearts and minds set? On work, the future, family, on the tasks to be faced tomorrow? But where is your heart and mind set? The degree that your heart and mind is set on Heaven is the degree that your heavenly life will increase on earth. We're not to set our hearts and minds on Heaven as an escapist strategy. We're to set our hearts and minds on Heaven because that is the only way God's heavenly life will flow out of us here on earth.

## FLOW OUT LIKE A RIVER

But having this heavenly life comes with an obligation. As it's His life, how do you think He would want it to be manifested? What's going to happen when you allow this heavenly life that the Spirit releases to you, to be loosed to those around you? Jesus explained it in John 7:38. This Scripture says, "Whoever believes in me, as the Scripture has said, rivers of living water will flow from within them." So this heavenly life is to flow out of you—and not just in a trickle. It is supposed to *flow* out like a river, but not any river. In the Greek, the word used here is *potamos,* and it's the same word Jesus used when in Matthew 7:25 when He talks of the man who built his house on the sand and then the "rain fell, and the floods came, and the winds blew" (NASB). So, this isn't a sedate little stream. This is a flood that, if you allow it, will overcome you as it flows out of you.

I want to link this river that Jesus spoke of with the vision of the river that Ezekiel had recorded in Ezekiel 47. Here is a picture of how the living waters are supposed to flow from within us. In this passage, the river comes from the heart of the temple, from the dwelling place of God. The dwelling place of God is now within us. He dwells within us by His Spirit, and the river is supposed to flow through us. If God's life isn't flowing through us, His people, who else is it supposed to flow through? There is no one else. God has no Plan B. We have been called for this very purpose.

There is no need to have to go to a meeting to receive a "fill up." We already have a well within us, from our innermost being, which should be continually flowing as a river. When we open the well and begin to allow the river of the Spirit, the heavenly life of God, to flow through us, it's just a trickle. As we flow in it, give ourselves to it, it gets deeper—ankle deep, knee deep, waist deep, and then a torrent we can only swim in—totally out of our control and totally into His control. It is His heavenly life, after all. This river is vast. It's not designed to satisfy you at the ankle level or at any other level until you are swimming in something that has no boundaries and no limits. No control! What an exciting prospect. Let's not seek to build dams or erect weirs. Let's just go with the flow!

What does it look like when it's flowing? What's its impact? Ezekiel 47:8-12 describes it:

> *...When it empties into the sea, the salty water there becomes fresh. Swarms of living creatures will live wherever the river flows. There will be large numbers of fish, because this water flows there and makes the salt water fresh; so where the river flows everything will live. Fishermen will*

*stand along the shore; from En Gedi to En Eglaim there will be places for spreading nets. The fish will be of many kinds—like the fish of the Mediterranean Sea. But the swamps and marshes will not become fresh; they will be left for salt. Fruit trees of all kinds will grow on both banks of the river. Their leaves will not wither, nor will their fruit fail. Every month they will bear fruit, because the water from the sanctuary flows to them. Their fruit will serve for food and their leaves for healing.*

Here's the picture of how the heavenly life Jesus has recovered for us will impact the earth. That which is dead or dying, under the influence of the kingdom of darkness, will be brought to life. There will be healing. That which is barren, will be transformed into fruitfulness. What is arid will be turned into places of rest and refreshment. Baca will be banished, because this river comes directly from the throne room, from the presence of God. Psalm 46:4-5 talks about "a river whose streams make glad the city of God, the holy place where the Most High dwells. God is within her, she will not fall." There is joy that comes with this river; and because it derives from God Himself, there will be permanence and sustainability about it that develops into a culture.

So, there is to be a culture of Heaven about you, flowing out of you. If not, you won't be any different from other good people around you. It's God's heavenly life in you that's supposed to attract the world, not your good, upright, religious earthly life. This is what God wants to do on the earth. He wants to restore it to how it was in the beginning. That's how He created it to be. This is why Jesus died. Everything God does on earth is geared toward this end. He wants His life to flow throughout the earth, so His glory is manifested. And He wants to do this through you. You are to be an example of His glory. It doesn't get much better than that.

But it isn't like a slot machine. It isn't just a matter of coming forward in a meeting, having someone put their hands on you, and you having some carpet time. Impartation is good, but that just opens the door. You have to take hold of it, as Timothy did. It's got to be your waking and sleeping cry, "God, I want more of You, and I won't let You go." That gets Heaven's attention. It was Paul's ultimate cry, even after years of missionary endeavor, "that I might know Him" (Phil. 3:10 NASB). Paul says he considers everything else as mere trash compared to knowing Jesus. That's what we're hungry for. And when we get hungry, encountering God merely in His deeds is not good enough. Yes, it's great to receive His benefits, His blessings, His goodness, His healing, His answers to prayers—but there's more.

Moses knew that. His prayer in Exodus 33:13-14 was 'If You are pleased with me, teach me Your ways, so I may know You and continue to find favor with You.' ...The Lord replied, 'My presence will go with you....'" David recognized this about Moses and wrote in Psalm 103:7, "He made known His ways to Moses, [only] His deeds to the people of Israel." How often are we like children who only see their absent father at McDonalds on Saturdays once a month. We know something of our father's deeds, his generosity, his good nature on those occasions, but because we don't live together, we don't really know our father's ways at all, who he really is.

Do you live together with your heavenly Father? Or do you just meet Him for 10 minutes each day and for two hours on Sunday in a religious version of McDonalds? If the latter is the case, you will know about His deeds, because He's always good, but perhaps not much about His ways, Himself. That is the better part. That is what heavenly life is about.

The people of Israel had a great chance to commune with God directly. God wanted the whole nation to gather before Him in the mountain. But the people chose to stay at a distance. Exodus 20:18-19 says the people "stayed at a distance and said to Moses, 'Speak to us yourself and we will listen. But do not have God speak to us or we will die.'

Are you choosing to stay at a distance, or are you hungry to go up the mountain and encounter Him and His Heaven?

## ENDNOTE

1. Martin Scott: http://3generations.eu/blog; accessed December 7, 2011.

# CHAPTER 6

## Jesus and His Kingdom

The first words of Jesus' public ministry as recorded by Mark in 1:15 are:

*"The time has come," he said. "The kingdom of God is near. Repent and believe the good news!"*

So, from the outset, Jesus made it crystal clear that the reason why He had been sent from the Father was to announce the coming of the kingdom of Heaven on the earth. Earthly life was not all God intended for human beings. He also wanted to imbue them with heavenly life.

The proclamation of the kingdom was His manifesto. Everything Jesus said and did was just expanding and clarifying the centrality of God the Father's Kingdom. The good news for the people was simple; you don't have to be in the kingdom of darkness anymore, with its poverty, its sickness, its victimization, and its oppression. You can come into the kingdom of light where there is healing, freedom, prosperity, and wholeness. This is the good news! Who wouldn't want it?

But as soon as Jesus had uttered this, He came under enormous and sustained spiritual pressure to divert Him from His mission. In Mark 1:9-13, some major events kick off. Jesus gets baptized. The heavens get torn apart. The Spirit of God descends like a dove (not as a dove). And the Father's voice booms out of Heaven. These are major supernatural events. There's amazing spiritual power here, more than any Old Testament event. The whole of the Godhead is involved and they're saying, "This is it, this is the time, the Kingdom of God is now here, on planet Earth, and it's going to be on earth as it is in Heaven!"

Then what happens? The Spirit drives Jesus into the desert to take everything satan could throw at Him. Jesus had to take it and overcome. Much was at stake. Saying that Jesus was tempted is quite a weak translation—the Greek word literally means attack. Satan attacked Jesus personally, and we know the avenues of attack he chose. And my guess is that there weren't just three occasions when He was attacked. If you know anything about how the enemy attacks you personally, you will know that he doesn't give up after three tries. I suspect that these were three themes of attack, probably lasting the whole 40-day period.

Luke then records that Jesus came out of the desert victorious and in the power of the Spirit. He went back to His hometown and to the synagogue at Nazareth. He preached from Isaiah 61:1, "The Spirit of the Sovereign Lord is on Me, because the Lord has anointed Me to preach good news to the poor." What was this good news? Freedom for the prisoners, recovery of sight to the blind, the release of the oppressed, the year of the Lord's favor. That is, God is on your side and is for you, not against you. And Jesus finished by saying, "Today this Scripture is fulfilled in your hearing" (Luke 4:21). My paraphrase is, "Today the kingdom of Heaven has come and it is here right now, as you listen to this."

And what happens next? Do they say, "Great! We've been waiting for this...at last some help." No. They try to push Him over a cliff.

This is attack and counterattack. There's a spiritual power battle going on behind the physical. The demonic realm is stirred up and severely rattled. So much so that demons seemed to spontaneously shout out who Jesus is, as soon as He showed up. "Have you come to destroy us?" they yelled out (Luke 4:34). Answer: Yes, He had. That's exactly why He had come. He had come to restore the original commission and authority to humankind, to do the job that they had been commanded to do in the beginning—to subdue the earth and bring the kingdom of Heaven on to the earth, under the authority of the Father.

Why is all this going on? Because Jesus is now revealed. What had been hidden in the physical after the Fall back in Genesis, is now incarnated. He's here. He's prepared. He's anointed. And He's a major threat to the whole edifice that the enemy has built up over centuries around the planet. The shadow boxing has now come to an end. The main event is now on. War has been declared.

Jesus proclaimed that the kingdom of Heaven is here. Effectively He was saying, "I'm going to take back what has been stolen. Everything that was lost by Adam, I'm going to restore; and I'm going to redeem humankind and bring them into the whole Kingdom of God." Here begins the real clash of the kingdoms. It's incredible that although Jesus proclaimed the coming of the Kingdom, although He modeled what it was all about, although He gave this mandate to His disciples, and although the early church carried on doing as they were commanded to do—yet only a few hundred years later, all this was almost totally lost!

Looking back in church history, we can see how effective the enemy has been in stealing the truth of the kingdom of Heaven and submerging it. I've already referred to liturgicalization of the Lord's Prayer that has exchanged powerful truths for a parroted, albeit truthful, liturgy. Here, familiarity has certainly bred ignorance. If overemphasis is one strategy the enemy uses, the other equally successful strategy is to push powerful truths to the margins. And teaching about the whole Kingdom of God has certainly suffered from this attack. We need to remember that the enemy attempts to focus our attention on the things that are visible, things of the traditions of earth. It is the *invisible* realm that is eternal. Paul says in Second Corinthians 4:18, that elements contained in the visible realm are temporary and *subject to change*. We know that the god of this world already has a large measure of control over that which is visible and of the earth.

To wrest that away from satan requires powerful manifestations of the kingdom of Heaven. Earth has nothing that can do the job. This is our job as children of God. We have the position and authority to change and restore much of it—if we bring the kingdom of Heaven into play. We live in a privileged generation because much of what has been pushed to the margins, lost, or simply ignored, is being restored. We know we're not going to see the fullness of the kingdom of Heaven in this Present Age. We know not everyone is going to be saved, healed, or experience full release in their lives. It didn't happen in Jesus' day either. Hebrews 2:8 says "in putting everything under him [Jesus], God left nothing that is not subject to Him. Yet at the present, we do not see everything subject to him.

Well, if that's the case, what can we possibly expect? Hebrews 6:5 talks about those "who have tasted the goodness of the word of God and the powers of the coming age." Although it's in the context of those who have fallen away, it clearly demonstrates that tasting the powers of the coming age is open to us. So the power of the kingdom of Heaven is not exclusively in the future. The powers of The Age to Come have penetrated This Present Age, and are for now. This is what is challenging satan's kingdom. Jesus demonstrated it. The disciples learned how to do it. The early church carried on doing it, and we are beginning to rediscover how to release it in our generation.

## WORDS AND WORKS OF THE KINGDOM

During his ministry, John Wimber repeatedly spoke about the importance of the signs of the Kingdom and that Jesus didn't just come with a message—He came with a ministry.[1] He not only proclaimed the Kingdom in words, but He brought the Kingdom with Him and manifested it in actuality. Jesus then gave His authority to the disciples to go and do what He had been doing. John 14:12 says, "anyone who has faith in Me will do what I have been doing" (NIV 1984). So, we have a mission to heal the sick, cast out demons, and preach the good news to the poor—the same ministry that Jesus had. We have the same Holy Spirit that Jesus had, and the same supernatural equipping.

Jesus didn't cheat and use power that we have no access to in order to fulfill His ministry. Everything He did, He did as a man empowered by the Spirit. He said on more than one occasion that He did nothing of Himself, but only what He saw the Father doing. Thus, our job is to proclaim the words of the Kingdom and do the works of the Kingdom. Both are essential. One without the other is not adequate. Jesus did both. We must do both.

It's a real disappointment that many expressions of church put the people of God into an audience, which results in passivity. God does not want an audience, rather an army. He wants people who know the spiritual authority they have. He wants people who live in faith every day, people full of the Holy Spirit, and people who know God's rule and reign, His Kingdom, running through the whole of their lives. He's not looking for perfection. Jesus is that already. He is our perfection. Sinners saved by grace will do nicely!

But instead of confidently looking to heal the sick, releasing those victimized by the enemy, freeing people up with prophetic words, and words of wisdom and knowledge, many find themselves unconvinced, timid, and fearful. They give the impression of not being very certain whether God will actually turn up at all when they step out. They act like soldiers, suspecting there's a war on, but desperately trying to ignore the draft and get back into civilian life as soon as possible. But we're all called to imitate Jesus. Are we going to give up and say these works of the Kingdom aren't for today? All this spiritual stuff has now stopped, and we're not supposed to be doing it? This is an excuse. I don't believe it is a thoroughly biblical position.

Of course, when The Age to Come arrives, the Kingdom will be seen in its fullness. Revelation 21:3-4 says:

*And I heard a loud voice from the throne saying, "Look! God's dwelling place is now among the people, and He will dwell with them. They will be His people, and God Himself will be with them and be their God. He will wipe every tear from their eyes. There will be no more death or mourning or crying or pain, for the old order of things has passed away."*

But for some, it will be too late. That's why we need to grasp our inheritance now.

## KINGDOM THINKING IS VERY DIFFERENT

It's probably a truism, but the kingdom of Heaven works in the way that God works. And the first thing we can say about how God works is that it isn't how we work. Isaiah 55:8-9 says:

*"For My thoughts are not your thoughts, neither are your ways My ways," declares the LORD. "As the heavens are higher than the earth, so are My ways higher than your ways and My thoughts than your thoughts."*

The characteristics of our Western way of thinking might be described as rational, logical, and largely evidence-based. We like to think that we live by the facts. So 1+1=2. Actually, we are much more emotional and instinctive about our decision-making than we often admit. But we do value things like fairness, equality, diversity, common sense, etc. However, the characteristics of God's thinking, God's ways, God's Kingdom aren't those things at all. It's no wonder we find it difficult to renew our minds as Paul urges us to do in Romans 12. The two realms of Heaven and earth have entirely different values.

The Kingdom of God is not known for its logic, intellectual prowess, or common sense. In fact, it transcends these natural characteristics. Rather, it is marked by the miraculous, the impossible, the inconceivable, and the back to front. For example, was it fair at the pool of Siloam that only one guy received healing? Was it common sense when wage rates for a whole day and for just one hour were exactly the same? Was it equal regarding talents when one person received 10, another 5, and a third only received 1? This Kingdom teaching by Jesus has very little to do with our ways and our thinking.

The Kingdom of God values what seems, in our human eyes, to be foolish and weak. Paul came to Corinth, in great weakness, yet in demonstrating the Spirit's power. Great results were achieved; whereas, at Athens where he had just been, he tried to use intellectual argument and got nowhere.

We need to remember that Heaven isn't a Western democracy where everyone is entitled to have their say and express their human rights. No. God gets to do what He wants, when He wants, with whom He wants, in the way He wants. So how, you may ask, is anyone supposed to run a business, family, charity, whatever, with the values of the kingdom of Heaven? How are you supposed to be an employee and see weak and foolish things provide breakthroughs? How are you supposed to help out at the local school, for example, and allow room for the upside down values of the kingdom of Heaven to influence decision making there? It doesn't make sense—to a mind conformed to this world's way of thinking.

Nevertheless, the Scripture is uncompromising. Yes, we can spin it this way and spin it that way to provide some wiggle room to justify ourselves. But the issue is not whether we can rationalize our way around it. Rather, if the Father has said it, how can we submit to it? And how will it work for us, in our situation? Father isn't going to change His ways, His thinking, His Heaven. It's all far higher, deeper, wider, and superior in every respect. No. It's we who have to change. Earth has to make way for Heaven. God has provided a way whereby that can happen. We have to have a mind transplant. Romans 12:1-2 tells us how to resist being conformed to this world by being transformed by the renewing of our minds—changing the way we think, and what we value.

All transformation, and that's what the Father is talking about, has to start with revelation. The penny has to drop. We can't renew our minds by effort or even by teaching per se. It has to be a revelation from God. The Holy Spirit has to drop truth into our minds; we have to receive it so we see where we didn't see before. Suddenly it becomes clear. It all makes sense. That, after all, is what good teaching is supposed to do.

You would probably agree that the way we operate routinely, is mostly if not entirely, conformed to this world's way of doing things. It's the way we were brought up, educated, and trained; and it leaves very little room for the ways of the kingdom of Heaven. You judge. In the past, has there been room in your business for the miraculous? Has there been consistent room in your family for the impossible? Has there been room in your workplace for signs and wonders? Has God had opportunities to bring success from what looks weak and foolish? So is your mind being transformed, or is it simply the same as those around you?

Bill Johnson says it like this, "God is our Father, and we inherit His genetic code. Every believer has written into his or her spiritual DNA the desire for the supernatural."[2] So, how hungry are you for this? How large is your appetite? Or is your mind already dismissing this as just not practical? Examine First Corinthians 2:9, "What no eye has seen, what no ear has heard, and what no human mind has conceived—the things that God has prepared for those who love Him." Here we are in our natural way of thinking. Of ourselves, our eyes, ears, and mental faculties are just unable to appreciate and understand, the comprehensiveness of what God has for us. But Paul isn't talking about unbelievers here, he's talking about Christians!

But he goes on to say in First Corinthians 2:10, "but God has revealed it to us by His Spirit." So, although in our natural state, we can't appreciate this stuff, we are able to by the Spirit of God. How? Verse 12 of that same chapter says, "What we have received is not the spirit of the world, but the Spirit who is from God, so that we may understand what God has freely given us." This text tells us that it is the Spirit of God who enables us to understand God, His gifts, His Kingdom, His values. This is part of what His job is.

But the text also tells us that we can easily allow the spirit of this world to dominate us.

Paul, in the third chapter of First Corinthians, calls Christians carnal who allow this to happen. Biblically, being carnal has very little to do with sex. It's all to do with not engaging with the Spirit of God whom we have been given. So this passage is saying that it is very possible to be a committed Christian and still not understand what God has for you. I'm not talking about the hereafter, but the here and now! God has made provision for you to understand what He's about, what His Kingdom is, what He has planned for you, now.

## KINGDOM TRADING

Jesus understood what He was to do because He knew who He was. We know from Scripture who we are, but that's about as far as it goes. We have not experienced who we are. It's still stuck in the pages of Scripture. Ephesians 2 expressly states that we sit in heavenly places. A heavenly place is a realm of dominion where authority is exercised. It is a seat of government. Jesus knew that it was His Father who sits in the highest place and exercises all authority and dominion. This is His throne.

Another way the Hebrews spoke of God's throne was in terms of mountains. Psalm 68:16 speaks of "the mountain where God chooses to reign." Psalm 99:9 exhorts us to "worship God at His holy mountain." It is to the mountain of God that we come—that's where His throne of grace is and that's where we come to trade our weakness for His strength, our sin for His forgiveness, our need for His grace. The mountain of God, the throne, is a place of divine trading.

I was first introduced to the concept of heavenly trading by Ian Clayton.[3] It took me a little while to get it. But it can be likened to a city exchange floor, but where we receive not what we have earned, but what Jesus has earned via the cross. This is the only kind of deal we can do with God in His Kingdom. We come with nothing, and He resources us on earth with Heaven's goodness and glory. This is what we do in intercession. We stand in the gap and "trade" the blood of Jesus for healing, salvation, and breakthroughs of every kind. His blood covers it all. It is the only thing in Heaven or on earth that does.

However, the truth is that we also do deals and trade with the enemy. This is what often prevents us from taking the knowledge that we get from Scripture and turning it into experience and life. Instead of using the resources of Heaven for our lives, we have all used the things of the enemy and become hooked. C.S. Lewis had a great insight when he created the character of Edmund in his book, *The Lion, the Witch, and the Wardrobe.* Edmund tasted the turkish delight that the white witch offered him, and he was hooked. It took the deeper magic of Aslan's death and resurrection to get him out of addiction and into freedom.

Just as Edmund didn't believe the stuff about Aslan, so we have not entirely trusted God. So we have made our own provision, just in case God doesn't show up—in case He let's us down. Adam and Eve traded unfettered communion with God and each other for fig leaves of disgrace, reproach, and guilt, because they didn't entirely trust that God was giving them everything.

Take the anxious thought, "I don't have enough." This doesn't lead us to begin trusting God for our finances. If we allow it space in our minds, it will begin to dominate, and we will begin to make our own provision. It invites a poverty spirit into our lives. It expands into jealousy for those who seem to have more than we do, and for whom money isn't an issue. It may lead us into spending on credit cards so that we appear to have enough, but we have no assets or income to cover it. Our minds begin to center on money and how to get more. We have agreed an exchange, a trade, but it has not come from the kingdom of Heaven.

Again, your boss, in order to get you to do something, indicates that if you do this and that, you will get promoted. It is manipulation. It is something for which Jezebel was known. It creates a hope inside you, and an activity outside that you otherwise would not have done. You are being controlled. You have yielded to it and have therefore freely agreed an exchange, a trade. But again, it has not come from the kingdom of Heaven. God has had nothing to do with it. There is now something at work in your life that has the power to govern part of it.

These strategies of the enemy, and many others, seek to use our lives to further their own agenda. Sometimes we willingly use their stuff, and other times we are fooled. Either way, it's all outside of the kingdom of Heaven and all outside of God's divine provision for our lives. C.S. Lewis' character, Edmund, is so deceived that eventually he allies himself with the witch's kingdom, in opposition to Aslan's kingdom. This is exactly how the enemy works.

Every trade, every exchange that is not in accord with Heaven means that the glory that you were given as a child of God gets diverted; and instead of being offered back to God, is intercepted by the enemy. He is forever seeking God's glory for himself. You must set your heart to come out of these exchanges you have made. They lead to death. God's grace will work with you to this end, even if it takes some time to work through.

It is the things we engage with, the things we touch, think about, work with—these are the things that govern our lives. These are our treasures, because they are what we do, think, and live with all the time. It is impossible to live with all these earthly things and think our real treasure is in Heaven. If it was, we would spend our time thinking about Heaven, engaging with it and being guided by it.

So sadly, most of our treasure is still on earth! It has no trading value in Heaven, only the blood of Jesus. But if you allow the Holy Spirit in you to work within you, there will be something rising in you that says there *must* be more than what I've experienced so far!

## Endnotes

1. John Wimber: Audio series, The Kingdom of God. Released by Vineyard Resources.

2. Bill Johnson, *When Heaven Invades Earth* (Shippensburg, PA: Destiny Image Publishers, 2003), 81.

3. Ian Clayton: http://www.sonofthunder.org; accessed December 8, 2011.

CHAPTER 7

# How Does His Kingdom Work?

To our way of thinking, the Kingdom of God is an upside down Kingdom. It is set up so that in order to receive, you have to give. That's just the way God has created it to be. So in order to live, you have to die. That's how it is.

Jesus was so immersed in the kingdom of Heaven that He actually believed that He had enough food to feed the more than 5,000 people who had followed Him and were hungry. It's how He thought. In the kingdom of Heaven, multiplication is normal. It's how God works. He gave thanks for what He had and immediately put Heaven's value on what was on the earth. Jesus didn't focus on what He didn't have. He isn't interested in what we haven't got. As Bill Johnson says, "He multiplies what we have, not what we don't have."[1]

God asked Moses what he had in his hand and it was just the rod he used as a shepherd, an ordinary instrument of his trade. Yet with a simple tool that Moses happened to have with him, God did amazing things. Similarly with Aaron's rod, God also did stunning things, and it became one of the objects of testimony that was continually in

His presence in the tabernacle. We do the natural with what we have, and He does the supernatural. So what have you got in your hand? Is it something you use every day? Can you believe that God can use it supernaturally and can multiply its impact in your life and in the lives of others?

What is on earth can now become subject to the laws of the kingdom of Heaven. It wasn't the words of the "grace" that Jesus said that made the difference. Saying grace is often, even among Christians, a ritual that moves nothing into a Kingdom realm. The key was that Jesus knew who He was and what authority He had in the kingdom of Heaven. He actually believed, He knew, that the widow was putting more money into the Temple treasury than all the rich people put together. He actually believed, He knew, that the centurion's daughter was sleeping and that He was going to wake her up and restore her to her family. He actually believed, He knew, that Peter could walk on water and that the storm was to be stilled.

Although Jesus had never read Romans 12:1-2, His mind was so renewed that He thought and believed in an entirely different way from everyone around Him. To Him, miracles were common sense, the impossible was rational, and the inconceivable was logical. No wonder the disciples didn't get it. So Jesus told many parables to His disciples, explaining how the Kingdom of God worked. Often, we mistakenly think that they are just stories to illustrate biblical truths. But they are a lot more than that. They are actually telling us how the Kingdom of God works. They are seeds directly from the kingdom of Heaven, which have the potential to germinate and reproduce.

The natural course of earth's ways will be to wash away Heaven's seed because it does not make sense. It is beyond all the parameters that earth has to understand it or assimilate it. If these seeds of the Kingdom are to be securely planted, nurtured, and harvested, some intentional cultivation is required on our part throughout the growth period. It doesn't happen overnight. In fact, earth will constantly attempt to reject Heaven's seeds because they will seem like foreign bodies. Just as a host body will keep trying to reject a transplanted donor organ, so Heaven's seeds will experience the same, and require continuous interventions from Heaven before they begin to flourish.

We can and need to continually live in a heavenly environment in order to keep earth's instincts at bay. These environments, cultures, and atmospheres are in total opposition to each other. Earth says feel first, then do what you feel, otherwise you are being hypocritical. Heaven says do what's right, and the feeling will follow. Hypocrisy, according to Heaven is not doing what is right. So, if you don't feel hungry for God, pretend! If you don't feel like praying, pretend! If you don't feel you are a child of God, pretend! Heaven's kingdom will soon respond to you and the feelings will follow.

## THE KINGDOM IS HIDDEN

In Matthew 13:33, we have the parable of the yeast, "The kingdom of heaven is like yeast that a woman took and mixed into about sixty pounds of flour until it worked all through the dough." What specifically was Jesus saying here? Simply, that although the change the kingdom of Heaven brings is an invisible one, it will always have a visible outcome. Yet at its core it is a hidden change, an invisible one, a supernatural one. The yeast, of course, is a picture of the work of the Holy Spirit, so it isn't of this world, of this realm. It is a heavenly work, not an earthly one. Nothing that doesn't have an invisible, supernatural core, therefore, can be of the Spirit, or of the kingdom of Heaven.

So, the Kingdom works in hiddenness. At least three parables reference this: the yeast in the dough, the treasure in the field, and the wheat and tares. Of course, this is completely at odds with how we work and how things work on earth. If we want something to be effective, we make it transparent. We comprehensively communicate. We use all avenues to make it visible. Not so in the Kingdom. Proverbs 25:2 says, "It is the glory of God to conceal a matter; to search out a matter is the glory of kings." There is a glory that accrues to God in the hidden. In His Kingdom, He has hidden many good things—not from us so we never find them, but for us in order that we seek and then we find. Deuteronomy 29:29 explains that "The secret things belong to the LORD our God, but the things revealed belong to us and to our children forever...." These secret things are not prohibited things. They are only things that have not yet been revealed. As we seek, God will allow us to find.

To take a simple example: it's like the traditional family Easter egg hunt. Parents hide the chocolate eggs, not because they don't want them to be found. On the contrary, they specifically hide them in places suitable to the child's ability to find them. So an Easter egg for a three-year-old would not be hidden at the top of a tree, rather on a coffee table in full view. On the other hand, if an egg was to be hidden from a twelve-year-old, it would take more of a hunt. But if the egg was not found and remained in secret, the whole reason for the hiddenness would have been lost. Heaven's secrets are there for us to find on earth.

So in this way, a Kingdom life is a discovery life. It may be that our minds can't conceive of this in the natural, but He will reveal it. He wants to reveal it. Things may seem hidden, but press in and God will reveal it by His Spirit. He will, however, not reveal it to those who are just vaguely interested. Jesus deliberately spoke in parables so that the vaguely interested would not find revelation. He confessed to His disciples that one of the reasons He chose to speak in parables was that He wanted to hide the truth from some. But to His disciples, those who left all to follow Him, He told them everything. He said in John 15:15, "...everything that I learned from My Father, I have made known to you." Whatever in the Kingdom you don't know about, press in for revelation. He will reveal it.

This is so that only those who really ask, receive; only those who really seek, find; and only those who really knock, have it opened. Have you given up because it didn't happen? Did you start well, asking, seeking, and knocking, but ran out of energy? Well, it's time to start again. You were on the right track. Declare an open heaven over your life, and set yourself to receive—like Daniel did. And even if the enemy tries to block, hinder, and steal, he won't be able to resist forever. Press in.

This is almost always God's way of working. Moses didn't meet God in the Egyptian palace. Rather it was in the desert—a hidden place. Joseph came from the hidden place of prison to become prime minister of Egypt. Gideon was also called from a hidden place. Hidden not only in the winepress, but as a nonentity in Israel. John the Baptist came from his hidden place, the desert, to announce the Messiah. Jesus Himself came from His hidden place of Nazareth to stun the nation. And many times during His ministry He hid Himself, sometimes even in the Temple. Paul needed three hidden years in the desert before he was ready for ministry. God often takes us through the hidden-exposure cycle many times in our lives to ensure our testimony; our ministry will last and we will find all the secrets that God has hidden for us.

This is the Kingdom we are inheriting. Whatever God is wanting to manifest around us and through us will come from the hidden place. Paul describes our life in Colossians 3:3 as being "hidden with Christ in God." Not only is it in a place far out of the enemy's reach, but it is so close to the heart of God that it is totally permeated with Him.

## THE KINGDOM MEANS CONFLICT

Although Jesus was a man of peace, everywhere He went He attracted conflict. He knew this was going to be the case and even said that He had come bringing a sword. He knew that the message of the Kingdom would divide even families. Someone has said that the Kingdom multiplies by dividing, and adds by subtracting! Certainly, the clash of the kingdoms was all around Him. His presence almost invoked it. Just getting up in the morning and mixing with people provoked some spiritual warfare.

Of course, there were different levels of conflict. One of the most interesting was His conflict with the religious (church) leaders of the day. Most of us prefer to avoid conflict, even if it means compromising what we know to be the right course, especially if our church leader or a well-known figure is involved. Jesus had no such qualms because He knew He had authority. In the rabbinical schools of the day, most rabbis taught without authority. It was every Jewish boy's ambition to go through all the stages of schooling and become a rabbi. Most never made it.

It may be that Jesus didn't spend all His years prior to ministry in the carpenter's shop, but in rabbinical school at an advanced level. The vast majority of graduates would be rabbis who taught without authority. They merely understood and passed on the traditions handed down to them. They were used to asking questions, important questions for sure, but not having answers. Jesus, on the other hand, was a Rabbi who taught with authority and had answers—to everything!

I've heard people label Bible seminaries as Bible cemeteries. I suspect what they mean is that they teach how the rabbis taught in Jesus' time. They teach what is already known, and ensure that good people pass it on to the next generation. Good as far as it goes, but inevitably it becomes a good system for maintaining the status quo. The desperate need today is for new leaders to get to a place where God can reveal more of the secrets of Heaven He has stored up for His people. We need men and women who know that there are new Easter eggs to find, and have an insatiable appetite to find them and expand the realm of revelation.

Paul says in Ephesians 6:12, "For our struggle is not against flesh and blood, but against the rulers, against the authorities, against the powers of this dark world and against the spiritual forces of evil in the heavenly realms." So criticism from religious leaders was nothing compared to conflict with the demonic. There were many occasions when Jesus provoked the demonic. Sometimes these were deliberate—the man from the Gadarenes—but often it was they who manifested voluntarily without Him doing anything, except being there. For example, the man with the withered hand in the synagogue in Mark 3.

But there are three specific instances where Jesus' response to the situation was the same; and, as John Wimber points out in his audio series on the Kingdom of God,[2] if grammar means anything at all, each of these incidents must have the same root cause.

First, in Luke 4:33-35, Jesus deals with what looked like a completely normal man in church. Jesus enters, and the man involuntarily cries out because demons have been provoked by Jesus' presence, "Go away! What do you want with us, Jesus of Nazareth? Have you come to destroy us? I know who you are—the Holy One of God!" I suspect he is not the only one who was amazed and even embarrassed at this revelation. However, Jesus rebukes them and they come out.

Next, in Luke 4:38-39, Jesus goes back to Peter's house that evening to find that his mother-in-law is sick with a high fever. Jesus has dealt with sickness before, and normally He just commands healing, saying: be healed. This time, however, He rebukes it, and the text says, "it left her. She got up at once and began to wait on them."

Finally in Luke 8:22-24, Jesus is crossing the lake with His disciples and He's asleep. A fierce gale of wind sweeps down from the surrounding hills and even seasoned commercial fishermen are scared to death. Jesus does the same thing again, "He got up and rebuked the wind and the raging waters; the storm subsided, and all was calm." Interestingly, Jesus was on His way to the demoniac in the Gadarenes to release him.

This is not to say that all normal-looking church people, all fevers, or all storms are demonically inspired. Clearly they are not. But some are, because these were. What's the point? The Kingdom works in a context of warfare. Now the devil isn't necessarily behind your car breaking down, or the kids being uncooperative, or you not being able to get a seat on the train. But if you're seeking to live in the Kingdom, you will see opportunities to press in to the enemy's territory each day. As you do so, you will know the pressure on you.

Demons do not play fair and we need to recognize that. For example, they are instrumental in giving you jealous thoughts, then they accuse you of jealousy! Often our reaction is to agree with them, sue for peace and give up, instead of pressing through. Job 22:21 in the English Standard Version of the Bible says, "Agree with God, and be at peace." The way of peace lies with agreeing with God, not with the enemy. The battle is there because you're doing right, not wrong.

The best way to overcome the pressure, is not to opt out of Kingdom living as some do. Rather it's to live a consistently clean and holy life, forgiving others, so that you yourself may be forgiven. Then, as satan had nothing on Jesus, he'll have not a lot on you. Now that might be easy to say, and often difficult to maintain. But to the extent that you can maintain it, you will walk in victory and avoid a build-up of demonic pressure in your life. So let's live in denial, and deny the enemy the opportunity to pressure us. We should remember that because the ultimate battle was victorious and permanent, every subsequent victory is permanent; whereas every defeat is temporary, and God gives us more opportunities to overcome.

Many Christians get so caught up with church life that they forget that there's a war going on. The front lines are not necessarily in the church, though sometimes they are. Rather, they are in our communities, on our streets, outside our pubs, etc. What goes on there isn't just social dysfunction, although it is. It isn't just drink and drugs, although it is. It isn't just antisocial behavior, although it is. There's a spiritual force behind much of it, urging it on. We have forgotten that our faith isn't an insurance policy, but rather a draft notice, calling us to the front line.

Some are desperately trying to be civilians and avoid the draft. God is not pleased. Jesus didn't die just to get us to Heaven. There's a job to do on earth.

Jesus never sought safe zones to avoid conflict. You cannot overcome what you do not face. So, we can do nothing of worth in God if we insist on seeking out and staying in the seemingly safe zones of our church buildings and our Christian communities. If we do, the enemy follows, and we find religious spirits manifesting that seek to convince us that somehow we are better than those outside, and we shouldn't mix with them. Yes, we may be blessed there, but we cannot insult God by asking for miracles for the already over-blessed, when He actually came to save the lost, the poor, and the dispossessed. God wants to move outside the walls!

## THE KINGDOM IS NOT IN OUR CONTROL

So, the way this Kingdom works is different. Unlike our world, it isn't the triumph of one set of arguments against another. It isn't the victory of one rationale against another or the superiority of one worldview against another. That's why you can never argue anyone into the Kingdom. The Holy Spirit has to reveal things to them. It isn't just a matter of inviting people to come to a church service, or giving them a good rationale about Jesus. The Kingdom of God goes beyond argument, rationale, philosophy, worldview, and culture. It isn't that one person is persuaded by man's wisdom to choose God over satan, or darkness over light. Something altogether supernatural takes place. A different reality altogether comes into play.

The Spirit of God does something within that we do not fully understand and is not at all in our control. It's like the wind, said Jesus in John 3, "You hear its sound, but you do not know where it comes from or where it goes." Yes, that's a picture of the Holy Spirit, but look at what Jesus goes on to say, "So it is with everyone who is born of the Spirit." You are supposed to be like that! There's supposed to be something at work within you that is like the wind, something you can't control, something not of you, something of Heaven.

Paul experienced this when he went to Cyprus. The consul Sergius Paulus wanted to hear the gospel, but the sorcerer Elymas was constantly whispering in his ear, you don't want to see him, it's all lies, etc. After a while, something of the Spirit of God rose up within Paul—a special anointing for the moment—and he found himself cursing the man with blindness. Pretty strong stuff. And immediately, darkness came over the man. Sergius Paulus believed. Paul had this experience on another occasion when he was with Silas in Acts 16. A female slave was earning a fortune for her owners by predicting the future through a spirit of divination. Again after a while of being provoked by her, something of the Spirit rose up within Paul and he publicly delivered her from her real demonic masters—and got a prison sentence for his trouble!

Can you remember an occasion when something, or rather Someone, rose up within you and you acted or you spoke? If you're living in the Kingdom, this should be your experience. This is how the Kingdom works. It's not logical or rational. It's God stuff. We need to redefine what's normal. Conforming to the world, to the visible, isn't normal for the Christian. It may be common, but it's not normal. God's idea of normal is how His Heaven works, not how the earth works. First Peter 2:9 says that Jesus has rescued us from the kingdom of darkness and brought us into the Kingdom of His marvellous light. This is now to be the norm.

But Jesus didn't just come to save us from darkness and bring us into His Kingdom of marvelous light so we can play church! He came to restore to those who have been saved, the authority and the power to demonstrate and manifest His Kingdom on earth as He had done. Power is the ability to do something and authority is the authorization to do it. We need both, and we have been given both, with the express intent that we partner with God in working in His Kingdom. So Jesus came not just to restore people to His Kingdom, but also to restore His Kingdom to His people.

This task requires more than words. Yes, we are to *speak* the words of the Kingdom, but we are also to *do* the works of the Kingdom. This isn't about helping an elderly person across the street, good though that is. These works include things that the unbeliever can't do. Sadly, we don't have very many models of this in the church today. While many are happy enough with speaking the words, the works are proving to be more difficult. There is no shortage of leaders who want to stand up and preach. There *is* a definite shortage of leaders who have the anointing to heal the sick, set free the oppressed, open deaf ears and blind eyes, and yes, even raise the dead. But that's what Jesus did; and in John 14:12, He said, "whoever believes in Me will do the works I have been doing."

Whether we're at work, home, or gathered together at church, we must always mix the Word with the works. It is this ministry that allows the Spirit of God to bring the Kingdom to reality in people's circumstances: physical, emotional, mental, or spiritual. Both support each other: the works demonstrate the truthfulness and authenticity of the words, and the words demonstrate the origin of the works. This is how the Kingdom works. When God wants to do something, yes, He speaks it out first. But His declared word is inevitably followed by the manifestation of that word in works. That's how we are to do it.

Jesus rarely asked people to believe just words alone. Remember John the Baptist having a wobble in prison? He sent his disciples to ask Jesus, "Are You the One who was to come, or should we expect someone else?" Jesus answered, "Go back and report to John what you have seen and heard" (Luke 7:20,22). What did Jesus say first in answer to this question? Listen to My marvelous sayings? Take note of My moving parables? What about My wise proverbs? None of these. Jesus said, "The blind receive sight, the lame walk, those who have leprosy are cleansed, the deaf hear, the dead are raised, and the good news is proclaimed to the poor" (Luke 7:22). Jesus told John's disciples to look both at the works and the words of the Kingdom. It was the same in the early church. "They devoted themselves to the apostles' teaching and to fellowship, to the breaking of bread and prayer" (Acts 2:42)—there are the words. "Everyone was filled with awe at the many wonders and signs performed by the apostles" (Acts 2:43)—there's the works. And the result: "the Lord added to their number daily those who were being saved" (Acts 2:47). Words with no demonstration of the truth are so much hot air.

But not everything that seems to be a good work is a work of the Kingdom. Not every work is in faith. Not every work is of the

Spirit. For example, say someone is upset and people come alongside him. They are kind, caring, and sympathetic. On a human level that's fine. We are human beings after all. But it's still human to human, flesh to flesh. Over and above that, the person needs something from God as well as something from you. No matter what the situation, we always need something from God! So the questions we should be asking, even as we hug the person is: What does God want to give to this person? What does He want to say to and do for the person?

If those questions don't arise in your heart, then you're not allowing the Kingdom to work. Everything you give is good, but there is also something better! Yes, Jesus also really cared for people on a human level. He was moved with compassion. He wept for them and with them, but He didn't stop there. He also knew that the Father wanted to give them more than mere human kindness. Consider the feeding of the 5,000, for example. Jesus had compassion on the crowd. He sat them down and fed them supernaturally. He gave something more than a human could on a human level, something that had within it the power to renew their minds and transform their lives.

There are many good people out there who are not Christians who do just as much human caring as Christians do—often a whole lot more! What makes something a work of the Kingdom, then? It is when, through you, God is able to do what He wants to do for them, when He wants to do it. That's what Jesus did. Jesus said that He could only do what He saw the Father doing (see John 5:19). The human, the physical, does have an important role. We can't *not* be human. It's how God created us. But alone, it's completely inadequate when it comes to working in the Kingdom. It's that wind effect rising up within us that is required.

Jesus said in John 6:63, "the Spirit gives life; the flesh counts for nothing." It is the spiritual, the Kingdom of God, His rule, that is the key to solving human problems. Because the Kingdom is God's rule, what we do is up to Him. It's His will, His timing, His method. Jesus said He could do nothing of Himself. So it is for us. But the

Scripture also says that in Him, we can do everything—nothing is impossible.

## ENDNOTES

1. Bill Johnson: http://www.bjm.org; accessed December 9, 2011.

2. John Wimber: Audio series, The Kingdom of God, released by Vineyard Resources.

# CHAPTER 8

# The Presence of Heaven

We should all beware when the Lord says, *I will be with you!* He said it to Moses as He sent him back to a hostile palace where he was already known, and from where he had fled years before to escape a murder charge. He said it to Joshua just before He told him to cross a flooded river with hundreds of thousands of people, with no prospect of any barges, boats, or bridges. He said it to Gideon just before He asked him to destroy his own father's Baal altar. No wonder Gideon asked for a sign! He also said it through Isaiah as He was talking about going through the flames of fire and passing through overwhelming waters.

The presence of Heaven is for a purpose. It isn't just nice to have. To be content with just a sense of God's presence in our Sunday meetings without an understanding what He has come for is folly at the very least, and dangerous at most. Such was the presence of the Lord that Adam and Eve hid themselves. They didn't want to have the discussion they knew was coming. Communing with God in the cool of the day without sin was a joy. Meeting Him with the presence of sin, however, was not going to be a happy experience. They knew better than we ever will this side of glory what the presence of Heaven was about. And they hid.

Psalm 97:5 talks about mountains melting like wax at the presence of the Lord. Judges 5:5 talks of mountains quaking at His presence. Leviticus 10:2 talks of fire coming out of the presence of the Lord and consuming Aaron's sons when they overstepped the mark. The prophet Nahum says that the whole earth "trembles at His presence, the world and all who live in it" (Nahum 1:5). Jeremiah in his Lamentations speaks of the presence of the Lord scattering the prophets and priests of Israel whose sin was to shed the blood of the righteous (see Lam. 4:13). In other words, the religious (church) leaders of the day, instead of shepherding the people, destroyed their very life by their own sin and weakness. Ominously the text says, "He will not continue to regard them" (Lam. 4:16 NASB).

In Solomon's Book of Ecclesiastes, he declares, "Do not be quick with your mouth, do not be hasty in your heart to utter anything before God. God is in heaven and you are on earth, so let your words be few" (Eccl. 5:2). There is no doubt that Israel's history had taught the people that the presence of God was powerful. Many knew that power only in judgment, but an exclusive few knew its joy and pleasure. In both cases, there is little call for man's words. The presence of Heaven doesn't call for self-expression, it calls for self-submission. Once submitted, there is an experience of knowing and being known that bypasses words. The presence of Heaven becomes married to earth, and the God who is in Heaven manifests Himself on earth to man.

The Book of Jonah is a personal testimony of someone sinning against and thus abusing the presence of Heaven. As a prophet, Jonah was anointed of God and knew His presence. In fact, Jonah knew of the tenderness of God's presence, even to the most wicked city in the known world, Ninevah. Although Jonah's political opinions were anti-Ninevah, God made it very clear that He wasn't interested in Jonah's earthly perspectives and sent him as His servant on a mission. But Jonah elevated his national prejudices above the heavenly presence of God. He thought God was wrong, and he was right. Jonah 1:3 tells of how he deliberately tries to flee from the presence of the Lord, as if the God of Heaven and earth only had jurisdiction in Israel.

We may have been tempted to let him go. After all, if he didn't want to go to Ninevah, why force him? He would not have been a very good prophet even if he had have gone. Why not look for someone else, someone who wanted to go, someone who might have done a better job. However, God doesn't think how we think. When He anoints someone and His heavenly presence rests on them, it is then set in Heaven. It is not easily let go. Romans 11:29 says of God that His "gifts and His call are irrevocable." For His part, He will never revoke what He has bestowed.

As children of God, He has called and anointed us with His Holy Spirit. As Romans 8:16 explains, the Holy Spirit is continually communicating with our spirits. Heaven's presence is upon us. It is irrevocable. God will continue to pursue us so that we live according to the presence of Heaven upon us.

Our continuing experiential deficit of Heaven's manifest presence must be a source of huge disappointment to the Father, particularly as the price for us to receive it was so high. But we have gotten so used to not experiencing the presence of Heaven, that we have created all sorts of mechanisms to compensate, both in corporate and personal experience. These, however, only serve to distance us more and more from the reality when His presence does come. So we have learned to live with the knowledge, but not the experience. How far the deliberate turning away from His presence is abusing the gift, I cannot say. But while God will not revoke His calling, I believe Scripture indicates that it is possible for us to revoke it by our actions. Ananias and Sapphira *lied to the Holy Spirit*. The heavenly presence on them that gave them their heavenly life left them, and there was no remaining protection for their earthly life.

## PRESENCE SHOULD BRING INTIMACY

But the presence of Heaven is not designed to put "the fear of God" into us. The heart of the Father is to commune with His people as He once did with Adam and Eve. He delights when His people come before His presence with thanksgiving and into His courts with praise" (see Ps. 100:4). He desires intimacy, and the presence of Heaven on our lives assures us of the Father's love and affection. Jack Frost, in his book *Experiencing the Father's Embrace,* speaks of the first time he tasted the presence of Heaven:

> It was then, when I was at the lowest place in my life, that I encountered the unconditional love of Christ for the first time. Instantly His presence broke the chains of alcoholism, drug addiction and pornography. In a moment's time, God gave me a new heart. The burden of sin lifted, and I felt true joy for the first time.... I had tasted of the Lord's goodness.[1]

Later he talks of equating the Lord's presence with *phileo* love. This is the "demonstrated, natural affection" that is what the presence of Heaven wants to bring. For him, the theology he knew had become the encounter he experienced.

Playing fast and loose with His presence was what the Old Testament people of Israel continually did. It is what led to their experiences of Heaven's judgment. This was and is, so far from the Father's heart, though. Even in Old Testament times, God revealed the fact that His thoughts for His people were tender. "For I know the thoughts that I think toward you, says the LORD, thoughts of peace and not of evil, to give you a future and a hope," says Jeremiah 29:11 (NKJV). A desire for intimacy, *phileo* love, is what will always emanate from His presence.

Those who did pursue God, found not only the love that flows from His presence, but the joy as well. David in Psalm 16:11 talks about God's presence being fullness of joy. In typical Hebrew couplets, he repeats the thought using different, even more powerful words, "with eternal pleasures at Your right hand." The Kingdom of God is a happy Kingdom. How sad that while one man could experience this, the nation as a whole consistently missed it.

But although Father has promised never to leave us or forsake us, the fact is the strength of His presence on us varies. If we, as Christians, are still walking in darkness, we are also playing fast and loose with His presence. We may be the people of God, as were His Old Testament people, but we are not immune from falling into the same traps they fell into. There's a difference between being born into the Kingdom of light and then continuing to walk in the light. The people of Israel were physically born into relationship with God. Heaven's presence was always there, available.

I often wonder how they could have turned away from Heaven's presence so often and so seriously, when God had done so many miracles for them, and His presence was so powerful with them. But then again, how much has God done for you and me and our families—and why is our outward person so different from our inward person? We have very little grounds to condemn God's Old Testament people. We have Heaven's presence dwelling within us, and still we make do without the intimacy that God offers. We have no time. We fall asleep. We have so much to do. There'll be another day!

Paul Leader was a Pentecostal minister in Wales, and wrote this in a recent blog:

> I think we need to re-evaluate our whole thinking on intimacy. It is about passion, and boy, do we need passion. But so often when we live in the realm of passion it just becomes a performance based relationship. How often and how long we pray, how much we read the Word, how often we serve others and do worship. There is a place for all that, but we need one thing more than anything else. We need to dwell. We need to just be. *Be still and know that I am God.* Realising that He is passionate about us before we do

anything, and no less passionate if we don't. We can dwell under the shadow of the Almighty, just dwell. We don't have to say anything when we get there. We don't have anything to prove. There is no song that we can sing that will turn Him on more. We need to learn to enjoy the silence. We need to be secure when He says nothing because He does not need to keep talking in this relationship. There was a time when I would strive to hear God's voice everyday and think that was a measure of approval and relationship with Him. Keep a prophetic diary of all that He said. If there was a day when I heard nothing I thought I was backslidden. We cannot measure relationship by that. In fact, real relationship is not measured by anything. It just is.[2]

As believers, not only are we called to continually live in the presence of God, we can't escape it, for He dwells with us and in us. God—the presence of Heaven, on earth. Because you're reading this book, the chances are that you are longing for a greater measure of His presence, believing that it will provide the answer to a quest for revival—and it will. But it has a cost. Even Job recognized that "a godless man may not come before His presence" (Job 13:16). He knew something of the presence of God when he was in his sinful state. And in Job 23:15, he admits, "I would be dismayed at His presence; when I consider, I am terrified of Him" (NASB). But under the New Covenant, our sinful state has already been wiped out. Yes, there are things still to be worked out, but your past sin, your present sin, and even your future sin has already been paid for. Heaven wants to presence with us, now. Yes, revival is great; a visitation is sorely needed, but Heaven's presence first needs a habitation. This is what the Lord says in Isaiah 66:1, "Heaven is My throne, and the earth is My footstool. Where is the house you will build for Me? Where will My resting place be?" And it isn't a church building, however magnificent.

## HONORING THE PRESENCE

It's time we learned how to honor and host the presence of Heaven. This is more important than our plans and strategies. Heaven's presence will hijack our plans and intentions if we will allow. In fact, as we respect and value what Heaven brings, we are more likely to hear plans and strategies that are Heaven-made rather than man-made. His presence can accomplish more in a minute than we can in a lifetime.

But we have camped at a place where we may have a sense of His presence during our corporate worship, but little sense of His presence outside of the walls. We have stayed far too long here. We need to break camp. It is time to move.

In our anxiety to more fully enter into His presence, sometimes we get sidetracked by trying to follow what this person says, or that ministry advocates. We go to a conference and do our best to follow the notes we bring back. This is good, but He isn't that difficult to encounter, unless we want it in a certain way and in a certain timeframe. Forget methods, systems, and programs. They may have worked for someone else, but don't be fooled into trying to put Saul's armor on. Coming into His presence is simple. Disciplining your flesh might not be. Don't concentrate on a method, concentrate on Him.

God had promised that His presence would be with Joshua. But on the other hand, Joshua was most probably advised by his military commanders, the professionals, about the best way to conquer the land and the cities in the land. I'm sure that God's revelation about how He wanted it to happen would not have received their immediate agreement. I have little doubt that Joshua had to overrule their advice many times, even after God's ways were proven. To earthly analysis, marching around a city for a week as a strategy for taking Jericho was insane. It made the people, as well as the army, vulnerable every day to aerial attack from the city, and did nothing for the morale of the people. The important thing was not that Joshua knew the promise of His presence, but that he continually honored that presence by acting upon it—in spite of the pressures around him. By so doing, Joshua was able to host the presence of Heaven, and that presence stayed on him.

Moses similarly knew that honoring the presence of the Lord was crucial. After he got his direction to go back to Pharaoh, he said that if God's presence did not go with them, then he didn't want God to lead them up from there. There was no way he was going back to Egypt without Heaven's backup. He also had God's promise to cling to, but he also had to act on it, even when it seemed stupid from an earthly point of view. Had he not done so, the promise would have been made void.

What's the good of Heaven's presence, if we ignore it when it conflicts with earthly ways? We need to allow Heaven access into our lives. We may say that we honor His presence in our church meetings on a Sunday. The test comes, however, not on Sunday, but on Monday when we are discussing the church budget! Are we willing to follow His presence and make Kingdom decisions that the "professionals" may not agree with? Or do we capitulate to the rational and earthly pressure of prudence and caution?

The presence of Heaven is never pressured and never in a hurry. Time is an earthly dimension, and while God recognizes time, He is not bound by it, hurried by it, or pressured by it. When we are, we move out of His realm and into our own. He will not be bound by commitments we give, even on His behalf, when we allow pressure and time, rather than His presence, to dictate agenda and decision making. Time is our servant, not our master. From God's standpoint, time can be stopped, even turned back in order to serve Heaven's purposes. We need to understand how Father treats time and, as His children, learn do the same.

## HUNGERING FOR HIS PRESENCE

How can we be sensitized to the presence of Heaven? In a word—hunger. The presence of Heaven is constantly seeking out the hungry. Hunger attracts attention in Heaven. It moves us to a place where we want Jesus in any way He chooses. God promises to draw near to us, when we draw near to Him. The onus is on us, because He has already done all that He's going to do. This drawing near is fueled by the desire for intimacy. Soaking in His presence enables us to hear Him in the whispers of our hearts. It allows us to eat and drink of Him. And we can have as much of Heaven's presence as our hunger allows, for God doesn't fill the satisfied, but the hungry.

Although he went about it in the wrong way, Jacob was hungry for the things of God. Esau the eldest, thought he had a right to the birthright and blessing, just because of birth. He was never really hungry for either. As far as he was concerned, it just came with the territory. It was his by right. This is a good example of how different God's ways are to ours. The cunning and conniving schemer who was Jacob, would have been run out of most of our churches for his behavior. Yet God accepted him, and promoted him to be a patriarch in the nation of Israel. So God says, *Jacob I loved, but Esau I hated.* Strong words, but hunger provokes God's love. To take God's things lightly, just as a right, provokes His great displeasure.

Often we don't know just how hungry our spirits really are. We have become so used to going to church without being hungry that we're not surprised or disappointed when we're not filled. God promises to fill only the hungry. When we do get a little peckish, we snack on secondhand God experiences, which have the effect of temporarily satisfying us, without having to put too much effort into it. Our immediate hunger is assuaged, and we think everything's fine. But our spirits are becoming hard. It takes longer and longer for the presence of Heaven to penetrate our spirits, and we become soulish. Religion is good at serving snacks, and it deadens our spiritual hunger pangs until we don't know they're there anymore. God, however, doesn't give out snacks. His intention is to accentuate our hunger more and more so that He can serve His whole banquet.

Smith Wigglesworth, in a pamphlet called *Faith that Prevails,* says:

> If you have lost your hunger for God, if you do not have a cry for more of God, you are missing the plan. There must come up from us a cry that cannot be satisfied with anything but God. He wants to give us the vision of the prize ahead that is something higher than we have ever attained. If you stop at any point, pick up at the place where you have dropped through, and begin again under the refining light and power of heaven and God will meet you.[3]

God isn't obliged to feed casual nibblers, and He won't. It's hunger that draws the presence of Heaven. If we don't hunger, we don't encounter the presence of Heaven; and because we don't encounter Heaven, nothing changes. If we did encounter Heaven, radical change must result—at least my Bible says it must. Everyone who really encountered God in the Scriptures was changed radically. Yet we claim to meet Him every Sunday, and change rarely happens!

But the banquet is always available. God never withdraws His invitation. Encountering His presence will open the storehouses of Heaven. James 4:3 says we do not have because we do not ask, and when we do ask, it is with soulish motives, not heavenly ones.

There is no doubt that our spirits, and maybe our minds, long for more of Jesus and His presence in our lives. That's good as far as it goes. But it's not enough. We also know that it is our flesh that powerfully resists. Why? Because it knows it will have to be crucified. Sadly, more often than not, it is the flesh that wins. But let's be clear, the flesh can masquerade as religious practice just as easily as it can manifest as sex, drugs, and rock and roll! So the flesh is just as alive in Christian leaders, who seek to maintain their hold over their congregation for their own identity, as it is in church members who seek to manipulate their leaders to support their own theology or doctrinal emphasis.

Church politics will quench hunger in whatever form it appears because it comes from earth. Real hunger engages with Heaven, not earth, and enables us to understand what the Father wants to pour out. His presence on us enables us to come into agreement with Him, aligning us with His heart. Praying through a list of our making, with no idea of what the Father wants to do, gives prayer a bad name. In fact, it has a bad name! We have reduced encountering God and His presence to "prayer."

There is an old hymn that declares that prayer changes things. No. It is His presence that changes the atmosphere in and over our lives that allows us to jigsaw into Heaven's plans and see Kingdom results. So it is His presence on the mountain that will bring breakthroughs and abundance in the valleys. It is the presence of Heaven that makes the difference.

Ruth Ward Heflin, in her book *River Glory*, says:

> God is doing things differently than we could have anticipated. He wants to encounter us in His way and is calling for a people who will accept His kingdom on His terms. Some have wanted to encounter God in their own ways. They are now becoming so hungry, however, that they are willing to yield to God's terms. Hunger makes you willing to yield to the presence of heaven.... God refuses to be our servant, to heed our every capricious whim. He is God.[4]

In the Anglican, Roman, and Orthodox traditions, it is the liturgy that has become central. In the Protestant non-conformist tradition, it is the preaching and teaching that is central. Everything leads up to the spoken message. It could be said that in many "new" Charismatic churches, worship is central. All have their place; but I believe God wants a "presence" culture to be central when we gather together. While all these other emphases may have been designed originally to facilitate God's presence, they mostly now bypass it and have become an end in themselves. We have to get back to a way of doing church that submits to the presence of Heaven.

A friend of mine, Helen, and member of the Your Kingdom Come team, posted this encounter with Jesus on a walk along Chichester Harbour Estuary in the United Kingdom.

> I began to ponder on the scents of heaven being released on earth and felt led to pray that God would release the scents of heaven in his church. I was drawn into the overwhelming Presence of God surrounding us which kept being magnified. Later on we passed an Australian Gum tree in a garden and as we rubbed the leaves their intense fragrance was released. We carried the leaves with us and each time I smelt their scent I could hardly walk as great joy and uncontained laughter bubbled up and overflowed. Staggering along the path or falling to my knees under the weight of his presence.
>
> I felt him say, "I release the scents of Heaven to increase hunger, to draw people to me to be fed with everything I want to give them. My fragrances will lead them to blessings of great joy as they discover the beauty of intimacy with me. I am passionate to share all that I am and all that I have with my beloved children. In the evening when darkness closes in and they can no longer see, my scents are heavy on the air and will draw them unfailingly to me their source. So it is in their lives when they feel as if they are in the dark and don't know which way to turn. Some of my children have lost their sense of smell they do not enjoy eating anymore and no longer feel hungry they are in danger of starving. Pray for their sense of smell to be restored for them to taste and see that I am good and for them to know the fullness of joy in my Presence."

Peter, on the day of Pentecost promised that "times of refreshing may come from the presence of the Lord" (Acts 3:19 NKJV). There is nothing more refreshing than a special fragrance. The church needs to smell the scents of Heaven once again, to be refreshed, to have its hunger on show again for Heaven to see. Only then will it be able to eat at the banquet that has already been provided.

## ANGELIC AS HEAVEN'S PRESENCE

There are many times in the Scriptures where God sent angels as messengers of Heaven to earth for specific purposes. Indeed one of the main revelations of Jacob's ladder in Genesis 28 is that angels seem to be constantly going to and fro, from Heaven to earth and back again, on missions for the Father. One of the exciting developments of the last few years is the increase in visible activity of the angelic. There is a definite quickening, an acceleration in Heaven's activity toward earth. If nothing else, it indicates that Heaven's presence is not just for soaking in, good though that is. There are missions to be accomplished—a Kingdom to be manifested.

Gary Oates, who has had dramatic encounters with the angelic realm, tells of an occasion when he was preaching in Maua in Brazil. He was preaching on the glory of God, when the presence of Heaven fell. He records in his book, *Open My Eyes, Lord:*

> People started crying. Some fell to the floor. My interpreter dropped to the floor, her glasses hanging off her face. The microphone had rolled out of her hand. The church's pastor came forward and tried to revive her without any success. Another interpreter came forward while I silently prayed what to do. "Do nothing," the Lord instructed me. "Watch what I'm going to do."
>
> Another wave came through the room more intense than the first. The third wave that came was so intense and thick I could not stand. I was somewhat stretched out with my arms holding onto the podium but my feet were like lead. I couldn't move my legs to keep me

from falling, and I started to slide down the podium. I lay on the floor over an hour and a half.

The pastor and all five of his assistants were on the floor. The meeting was left completely in God's hands. People were crying out. Tears flowed freely. Many were on their faces as pockets of God's glory touched people in various parts of the building.[5]

None of this was to give people a "sense of His presence." This was real, and in many cases, terrifying. When the presence of Heaven comes, holiness comes, majesty comes. Healings and other supernatural encounters happen. People are changed. Their lives are turned upside down. How dare we say we meet the presence of God each week. If we haven't changed, we haven't met Him. Jacob wrestled with the angel of the Lord all night refusing to let go. He was hungry. And because he would not give up, something of Heaven was birthed in him that transformed his life. He might have thought, *Well I've had the blessing from my father, no need to struggle.* But Jacob would not give up until he had the blessing from God Himself. Let's not settle for something less than our inheritance.

Daniel had been seeking the presence of Heaven for three long weeks before Heaven was manifested in front of him through an angel. Daniel 10 records that this visitation of Heaven was personal. Those with Daniel as he walked along the Tigris did not see anything, but were overcome with terror and hid themselves. Even Daniel himself had no strength, his face turned pale; he records that he was absolutely helpless. At one point, he confessed to the angel that he could hardly breathe and couldn't talk. He fell into a deep sleep before the angel delivered the heavenly message and spoke strength into him.

A similar experience was had by the apostle John on Patmos. In this case, it was a vision of Jesus Himself. John fell down as dead. This was no reverential bow, no courtesy to a long lost friend. John had completely lost all control over his body. He was totally overcome and undone. We know something of the power of the sun in our ozone-depleted atmosphere, which means that we have to put sun block lotion over our bodies to prevent skin cancer. But this was something else, something that sucked the very life out of John's earthly body. This was the presence of Heaven.

Here is another story that Gary Oates recounts from Brazil. This time in Manuas. A girl, Rachel Stoppard, followed Gary's instructions to look. This is what she saw:

I turned around slowly and what I saw first were chariots of fire all along the back wall. As I followed this around, I glimpsed a huge angel standing behind me and suddenly fire was shooting out of him. It so caught me off guard that I fell into a chair, but the angel caught me.

As he did, this fire shot from him into me starting at my head. It was like electric waves of fire in my head proceeding on down to my arms and to my legs. It was like wave after wave of this slowly pulsating through my body. I wanted to scream because I thought I was going to die as this fire went through me. As a wave would go through, I could feel the angel's arms around me tightening up and saying, "Just relax. I've got you. You're not going to die." He held me and kept saying, "I'm not leaving...I'm not leaving."

In the process of all this happening, I started becoming aware out ahead in the distance I could see the throne room. As I started focusing on the throne, I began crying, "Take me...I want to go there. I want to go there." I could see the soft light pulsating off the throne and I could see the colours swirling and moving. Finally the angel said, "No, it's not time yet. You are to stay here." Gradually the picture before me began to fade and I became aware about four hours had passed.[6]

## INTIMACY AND OBEDIENCE

John 14:23 makes very clear on what terms Heaven's presence will be manifested:

> Anyone who loves Me will obey My teaching. My Father will love them, and we will come to them and make Our home with them.

Intimacy (anyone who loves Me) leads to obedience (will keep My word). The result is that we will receive not only the Father's love, but His continuing presence. Abiding suggests a pleasurable continuance, just as a loved friend would come to stay for a while at your home.

Unfortunately, much teaching on obedience has owed little to the presence of heavenly intimacy, but rather the presence of earthly rules and a works-based reading of Scripture. The very word obedience somehow seems to dispel the notion of intimacy. This is primarily because obedience is preached and seen as a servant issue. Congregations are told to obey their leaders, children to obey their parents, even wives to obey their husbands—and little of it derives from intimacy. It's all because it's the "right thing to do," and by the way, the Scripture says it—so just do it! This places us as servants; but we are not just servants, but sons and daughters who serve.

This distinction makes an enormous difference and is worth exploring because it has taken us away from an emphasis on intimacy, and on to "doing things" for the church. This means many of God's people have been severed from any awareness of the presence of Heaven in their lives. What is important to the local church has been getting people to do the crèche, the coffee rota, welcoming, singing, children's ministry, and so on. Servanthood has been preached as a recruitment mantra to get people to do jobs. The promise is that if you are a "faithful servant," you will enter into the joy of the Lord. Unfortunately, the joy of the Lord is about intimacy and this servant-based, task orientation has the effect of taking away any time or motivation to seek the presence of Heaven.

Of course servanthood is a biblical doctrine. But it has been so exalted that we actually think we are servants. We now pray like servants, "Please, help me, Lord. You say the word, and it will be done." The implication being that whatever I say is worthless because I have no authority. John 15:15 states very clearly that God no longer calls us servants. Father has myriads of servants—angels. He doesn't need any more and didn't create us in the first place to serve. Adam's mission was to subdue and rule. Yes, Jesus came to serve, but He served as a Son, not as a servant!

It has been one of the highest accolades that Christians have been given as they retire from active church work—they were faithful servants for x years. There's nothing the flesh likes more than jobs to do. It means there is little time to spend in the presence of Jesus. No wonder few people even know how to spend longer than an hour in God's presence.

If most church leaders had their way, such serving would occupy most of the waking moments of each and every member of their congregation. We are now a generation who know how to set out the chairs, but feel impatient if we have to spend time in a meeting waiting on God, especially if He doesn't say anything within the first 30 minutes. The presence of Heaven is now a theoretical concept, rather than a practical reality. Many of us have had years and years stolen from us. Tommy Tenney, author of *The God Chasers,* put it like this:

> It is time for us to learn that our programs are not progress. What we need is presence. We decide that whatever it takes and wherever it comes from, we must have Him. And He wants to come on His terms, not ours. Until then, the absence of "awesomeness" will haunt the church.[7]

Let's remind ourselves that the obedience that counts in the Kingdom of God is that which derives from intimacy. Obedience that derives from any other source is counterfeit. The Pharisees were great on obedience and it proved to be a weighty yoke around the necks of ordinary folk who simply wanted to know what to do to be right with God. Their traditions and teachings led generations astray and caused Jesus to call them "whitewashed tombs" (Matt. 23:27). They looked beautiful and beyond criticism on the outside because they could point to the commandment. But on the inside, where intimacy is measured, they were "full of the bones of the dead and everything unclean" (Matt. 23:27). John sums this up in his letter. Second John 1:6 says:

> *And this is love: that we walk in obedience to His commands. As you have heard from the beginning, His command is that you walk in love.*

The true walk of obedience comes from heartfelt love.

## ENDNOTES

1. Jack Frost, *Experiencing the Father's Embrace* (Shippensburg, PA: Destiny Image Publishers, 2006).

2. Paul Leader, *Perspectives*, hosted by Martin Scott; http://3generations.eu/blog/.

3. Smith Wigglesworth, *Faith that Prevails* (Springfield, MO: Radiant Books, 1966), 15.

4. Ruth Ward Heflin, *River Glory,* 15.

5. Gary Oates, *Open My Eyes, Lord* (Moravian Falls, NC: Open Heaven Publications, 2004), 85.

6. Ibid, 91-92.

7. Tommy Tenney, *The God Chasers* (Shippensburg, PA: Destiny Image Publishers, 1998), 18.

CHAPTER 9

# The Power of Heaven

Sid Roth, well-known Messianic Jew, author, and radio host, in one of his broadcasts, recounts some of the power stuff from the early church that God did through the apostles, and asks where has it gone. If God is still the same, yesterday, today, and forever, that must include the 21st century. So where is it? If God hasn't done the changing, who has?[1]

Many Christians have been too content to keep the power of God within the realms of the Book. They're happy to read about Elijah running so fast that he overtook a chariot—that's fast. They're happy to read of Philip being transported to somewhere miles away from where he was in an instant of time—that's really fast. They're happy to read of Jesus having angels physically appearing and ministering to Him. Yet if this is taken out of the Book and talked about happening today, people look at you funny!

New Age advocates are happy to demonstrate a power that doesn't come from God, and many are attracted. Christians seem to feel that the right approach is to stay well away from this kind of thing. However, Moses didn't feel that at all. When Pharaoh's magicians threw their rods down and they became snakes, and vice versa, Moses didn't walk out because they were using demonic power. He was happy to continue to demonstrate the superiority of Almighty God over the demonic. And so were Joshua, Elijah, Elisha, Daniel, Peter, and Paul.

So why do so many Christians and Christian leaders just want to stay away from such encounters? Perhaps because they don't feel they have any of God's power within them. They are happy to teach, preach, argue, and debate. But First Corinthians 4:20 says, "For the kingdom of God is not a matter of talk but of power." But power on earth does not give you power in Heaven. However, power and influence in Heaven will most definitely give you divine power and influence on earth.

## How Much Power Is at Work in Us?

What did the early church have that we don't have? What did they understand that we don't understand today? There is a well-known verse that has a revelation for us when it comes to understanding God's power. It is Ephesians 3:20.

> *Now to Him who is able to do immeasurably more than all we ask or imagine, according to His **power** that is at work within us.*

Look at this closely. We know God is able to do immeasurably more than we can ask or imagine. There's no doubt there. But look at how He does it. It is *according to His power that is at work in us.*

What does *according to* mean? My thesaurus says, in accordance with, in proportion to, conforming to, complying with, consistent with, corresponding to. So what Paul is saying is that all this from God only gets manifested according to, in proportion to, consistent with the measure of power that is at work in us. So the crucial question: what is the measure of power at work in you? We know that potentially, it is as it was with Jesus. We have the same Holy Spirit indwelling us. But we also know that some people seem to have a lot more of God's power on them than others. Now this might be an academic question for some, but not for those who are hungry for more of God.

It means that everything we receive from God is in proportion to the measure of His power at work within us. It isn't according to the amount of praying we do, although praying is helpful. It isn't according to the degree of serving we do, although that's a good attitude. It's about the degree of God's power at work in us.

God can do all you can ever ask or imagine. That isn't in doubt. That He wants to lavish it on you also isn't in question. The real issue is why does it not seem to manifest in us? And this verse in Ephesians says it's all to do with the degree of divine power that is working in your life.

There is no doubt that Jesus displayed the power of the kingdom of Heaven in His life. We've already seen that His very presence was sufficient to expose darkness and bring in the Kingdom of God. As mentioned previously, in Mark 1:24, Jesus goes into a synagogue and by just being there, provokes a demonic manifestation, "What do You want with us, Jesus of Nazareth? Have You come to destroy us?" So what happens when you show up in a room? God's power is manifested by His presence. He just has to show up. Whether it was to Moses on the mountain at Sinai, to Paul on the road to Damascus, or to John on Patmos, His very presence means His power is available within you.

Wherever people in Scripture met God or His angelic messengers who reflected God's presence and glory, they did not remain the same. They changed. For Moses, God's full glory emanated from His face such that the people told him to cover up. For Isaiah, he felt totally undone. John fell on his face as though dead. Paul was temporarily blinded.

Has God changed? Why is His power not evident today? We can echo Gideon's frustration in Judges 6:13:

*...if the LORD is with us, why has all this happened to us? Where are all His wonders that our ancestors told us about when they said, "Did not the LORD bring us up out of Egypt?"*

## A SENSE OF POWER

I want to suggest that His presence is not really evident. We've become content with a "sense" of His presence at our Sunday meetings, and we go to our Sunday lunch satisfied that we had a good time. But if it's His presence that brings His power and all we're getting is a sense of His presence, all we're going to experience is a sense of His power. That might suffice if you're seeking to comfort someone; but will not suffice if you're praying for healing from cancer. A sense of His power will not suffice if you're seeking deliverance for someone. It will not suffice if you're seeking to break the power of drink, drugs, or anything else that has taken over a life.

We need more than a "sense" of God's power. We need to know His dynamic power at work within us. In Acts 1:8, Jesus clearly said, "you will receive power when the Holy Spirit comes on you." Was Jesus talking about just a sense of His power? Do you think Jesus was referring to just a pinch of power? Was His promise just talk, or was He saying that we would have the same power He had? Luke 4:14 records Jesus returning to Galilee from the temptations in the desert "in the power of the Spirit," to begin His ministry. And from the outset, everyone saw it was a fullness of power.

It is the Holy Spirit's desire that we come to the place where He is able to fully operate in our lives, as He did with Jesus. This is meant to be our inheritance. Some will say we can't do that, for Jesus was without sin. Clearly, a continuing lifestyle of sin and grieving the Holy Spirit will certainly mean that His presence, and therefore His power, will be minimal in our lives. But Jesus did say in John 14:12 that "whoever believes in Me will do the works I have been doing." He didn't say you had to be without sin to do it. The disciples certainly weren't without sin.

The Pharisees always get a bad press because of their legalism; but to be fair to them, they were people of the Word, albeit the Old Testament. It might be stretching things a bit to call them the evangelicals of their day, but they taught the Word, they preached it, they even made some of it up themselves! But they never found the power or the life in it.

Second Timothy 3:5 talks of people "having a form of godliness but denying its power." Paul says, *have nothing to do with them.* Why? Because it is so easy to get caught up in doing exactly the same. Talking about something might be a form of godliness, but with no power to implement the talk is a certain route to increasing disappointment, not increasing power. Yes, contending for manifesting the power of God is a tough journey. No doubt about it. It is much easier just to talk about it, sing about, even pray about. There is no shortcut to the power of God in your life. There are no spiritual laws that, if you obey, you can shortcut your way to more Kingdom power in your life.

## GOD HAS ALREADY POWERED YOU UP

If you want to begin, or continue this journey to see God's power manifest more in your life, then you need to begin by looking at how the Holy Spirit works to give opportunities to grow in the power at work within you. In Exodus 4:21, "The LORD said to Moses, 'When you return to Egypt, see that you perform before Pharaoh all the wonders I have given you the power to do.'" So God requires you to begin to perform what you have already been given the power to do. Moses had been called of God for a purpose. But before the main call on his life was revealed, he had an initial task to perform that would both test him and equip him. God required him to demonstrate Heaven's power in front of Pharaoh and his magicians. To position Moses for the full deal, he had to use the power God had already given him, even though he didn't think he had been given any power. Not too different from us!

You have been created for a purpose. You have been called by God for that purpose. Your destiny, shape, and gift mix has a uniqueness found in no one else. Stop trying to be like others and find out about your own God-given destiny. You will discover the measure of power that God has already put within you. Of course you might not yet know what God's destiny is for your life, but God doesn't impose His destiny on you. It's not a rigid thing. He loves to give you the desires of your heart, and the desires of your heart are somehow woven into His great purpose—as you fulfill your desires, He fulfills His purposes.

So a good place to begin in understanding what your life is about, is to ask yourself about the desires of your heart. Not what you've stumbled on, not what you've been asked to do, not what you do just to fill in the gaps of what others are not doing and just needs to be done. Too many Christians spend their whole lives doing these things and never find out what they were called for. No; what do you love to do? What do you feel you have been created for? It's in that arena where God wants to show you His power.

Gideon needed to find out the same thing. The angel of the Lord or what he supposed was the angel of the Lord, appeared to him and talked with him. After Gideon had answered, listen to what the Lord told him, "The LORD turned to him and said, 'Go in the strength you have, and save Israel out of Midian's hand. Am I not sending you?'" (Judges 6:14). It turned out that it was the Lord Himself who appeared to Him and said the fact that He was sending him, and that means Gideon already had the strength and the power to go—even if he don't recognize it. Again, it was in the arena of God's purposes for Gideon that God wanted to show him the power he had been given.

Now we must ask,

## WHAT KIND OF SPIRIT RULES?

In Second Timothy 1:7 Paul contrasts power with timidity. God did not give us a spirit of timidity, but a spirit of power. Do you have a spirit of power or timidity at work within you? Let's imagine we are going out on the streets to do some treasure hunting, which means that you're going to approach strangers with the aim of offering to pray for them. What are you feeling? What thoughts grip you?

Here's what my thesaurus says timidity can mean: first it can mean fear, horror, panic, trepidation. Second, it can mean weakness, diffidence, reserved, reticent. Third, it can mean shyness, nervous, tense, worried. You may identify with all of them, or just one. Whatever, it can be overcome and needs to be if you want to exercise the power God has already given you. The verse in Second Timothy 1 says timidity doesn't come from God. So to carry on allowing timidity to rule over you, however it manifests, will immediately stop God's power at work within you. So it's important. Nothing is supposed to rule in your life except the kingdom of Heaven, which is God's rule.

But we are all in good company. Many of God's leaders, like us, began with a spirit of timidity. Moses did. When God challenged him, he had one excuse after another. Gideon was the same. This mighty man of valor was hiding for fear of his enemies in a winepress, which was a hole in the ground. Don't look at your timidity as a barrier, but rather as a locked door to which you already have the key. Deliberate and intentional acts of timidity-denial will unlock the door; and once opened, these acts will release your destiny and the spirit of power that God has already given you.

## TEST IT OUT

God is fine with you testing out what He has given you. Moses wanted to test it out, and that was OK with God. Remember the rod turning into a snake and the leprous hand? Gideon also sought to test out his call with fleeces, as did Peter. He got out of the boat and walked on water. God has no problem with us testing out the power He has given us. He does, however, have a problem with us just talking about it, but doing nothing. As First Corinthians 4:20 says, "the kingdom of God is not a matter of talk but of power."

The testing out that both Moses and Gideon asked for wasn't about clarifying what God had asked them to do. Understanding wasn't the issue. Both knew what God wanted of them. They knew the implications. That was the problem. For Gideon, it meant destroying his father's idols and potentially being thrown out of the household. For Moses, it meant going back to where he had committed a murder and risking being caught. Both of them had to decide—did they want to risk God's way, God's power, or was it all too much?

For us, it's not about Bible knowledge or theology. The question is rather, will we risk opening ourselves up to God's realm, to His way of doing things, to stuff that is impossible, inconceivable, unattainable, and unthinkable. That's the sort of stuff God does and wants His disciples to do.

Moses didn't know that the snake was going to turn back into a rod. He didn't know that his leprous hand would be healed. Gideon didn't know that just 300 men would win a battle against a vastly superior enemy. Joshua didn't know how putting all his trust in a foreign prostitute, Rahab, would turn out. Peter didn't know how his episode of walking on water would turn out. He could have drowned. Paul didn't know that his blindness on the Damascus road was only going to last for a few days.

When you put your life in the hands of God, you have to trust Him, because you don't know how it will turn out. But you do know that He is good! He loves you and wants you to achieve everything that He has created you to accomplish.

Because His ways are higher, different, and superior to ours, what you may think is a good plan, God might not. What you think will advance His Kingdom, might not be the option that He takes. He just might do something, or want you to do something that you think is foolish, or weak, even absurd, ill-advised, maybe imprudent, perhaps unreasonable, and crazy. Are you up for that? Will you trust Him whatever? Will you allow Him to show you His power in your life, in His way?

Most Christians won't, most churches won't! They want to re-main safe and in reasonable control. Consequently, they will never know the power that could be at work within them, because God isn't reasonable, in their terms.

## WHAT DOES GOD'S POWER LOOK LIKE?

This is where we often miss it. On earth, power means force, might, muscle, the ability to control and command, maybe to dominate, perhaps making decisions that others have to follow. If someone has those things, we say they have power. Now we might believe we don't think this way, but actually we do. The disciples certainly thought this way. It comes straight out of the Old Testament. In Luke 9:54, the disciples wanted to call down God's power, "When the disciples James and John saw this, they asked, 'Lord, do You want us to call fire down from heaven to destroy them?'" They were probably thinking about Elijah, when he called fire from Heaven to consume the sacrifice at Carmel. Or maybe they were re-calling Elisha, after he called a bear to set upon some lads who were calling him "baldy." It is the way we have been taught and the way the media communicates to us. Thinking in this way has become second nature to us. Earth's ways are embedded in us. But it is not the way of the kingdom of Heaven.

That is not to say that God doesn't have all this potential. All this capacity and strength still exists within Him and the New Testament confirms this. Hebrews 12:29 says, "for our God is a consuming fire," quoting Deuteronomy 4:24. So God hasn't changed who He is, but He does change how He deals with us. The Old Testament was all about reminding people how sinful they could be and were. It was about how much they needed a Savior. Now that the Savior has come, God wants to bring in His heavenly kingdom, and thus the power God uses to bring in His Kingdom is very different.

This was precisely the reason why Jesus taught the parables of the Kingdom—so the disciples might be drawn out of their Old Testament mindset and into a New Testament Kingdom mindset.

It was difficult for them, and it is for us. Remember the widow's mite. Jesus said it was more than all the rest put together. Was that a little bit of sentimentality to encourage the widow, or was that a real and actual measure of Kingdom values? Was it really actually more in Kingdom terms? Yes. Jesus was saying that there was more Kingdom power in that mite than in the thousands of other coins that the rich put in. Our mindset has to change. Our churches and bank accounts are still being budgeted according to the world, not the Kingdom. God supernaturally multiplies mites! He doesn't need to multiply the thousands. No faith needed for that, and therefore no value in the kingdom of Heaven.

In Matthew 13, Jesus explained the power of the Kingdom to His disciples in this way:

> *The kingdom of heaven is like a mustard seed, which a man took and planted in his field. Though it is the smallest of all your seeds, yet when it grows, it is the largest of garden plants and becomes a tree, so that the birds of the air come and perch in its branches* (Matthew 13:31-32).

So here is the power of the Kingdom. Something small and really insignificant in earthly terms grows into something large and really significant in God's hands. Why? Because the power isn't in the item or person. The power is in the one who owns the item, or rules over the person. Paul expands on this in First Corinthians 1:27-28:

> *But God chose the foolish things of the world to shame the wise; God chose the weak things of the world to shame the strong. God chose the lowly things of this world and the despised things—and the things that are not—to nullify the things that are.*

So what power can you expect God to manifest in your life? What sound is going to come from Heaven for you? The sound of God varies according to what He wants to accomplish. Adam and Eve heard the sound of God walking in the Garden in the cool of the day. At first it was a welcome sound, not so later. David heard the sound of marching in the tops of the balsam trees.

It was a call to action. Ezekiel heard the sound of many waters. Elijah heard a still small voice; John heard a trumpet voice; and the 120 disciples ensconced in the upper room heard the sound of a rushing mighty wind.

Often, it will be the still, small voice, the impression, the fleeting thought, that if you act on it in faith, will transform something of little value into something of immense value to the Kingdom. That is not to say that this will necessarily be of immense value in the world's eyes! So what's our problem? Simply, that we don't hear the voice, the impression is overwhelmed, and the fleeting thought fleets! When we do hear the voice, we sometimes dismiss it. And if we don't altogether dismiss it, we display a spirit of timidity and are very reluctant to do anything that will embarrass us or make us appear foolish. Unfortunately for us, this is how the Kingdom works—and God isn't going to change. He requires us to live by faith. That means risking that our hearing, our discernment, might be wrong. It means agreeing to appear silly, maybe losing our reputation for being sensible and mature, and maybe doing ridiculous things. It means being accountable to God before being mindful of others.

Israel had an opportunity to see God's power on Mount Sinai. God intended not only that Moses draw near, but that the whole nation should. But they were afraid of getting so close to a God they couldn't control. It was not the reaction God was looking for. God wasn't just looking to *show* His power, He wanted to *share* His power. He wanted a people on whom His power could rest. It was what He had created the nation of Israel for. Their fear was one of the many reasons for the lack of power on the nation of Israel.

The Body of Christ is the new Israel and God is still looking for a people on whom His government and power can rest. Unfortunately, there are probably just as many reasons why we lack the power God wants to rest on us.

One of the reasons for such a lack of power is a very simple one. James 1 says that a tongue out of control renders faith worthless. That person is not going to attract Heaven's attention. If blessing and cursing come out of the same mouth, it is reflecting what's inside. God isn't going to give His power to someone who can't control their words. James says it's the same as being polluted by the world. This isn't just a matter of the odd "swear word." What the Scriptures are highlighting is a heart attitude that refuses to bless. It means that the heart is self-oriented, and not looking out for other people.

Self-orientation is how the world works. It's how governments work. It's about what is in the national interest. It is how unions, businesses, media, charities, and even some churches work. Cursing can be interpreted as the absence of blessing. If we have a blessing to give (and we do), what happens when we don't release it? It may be because of thoughtlessness, embarrassment, being judgmental, or even because of our own frustration—whatever.

Another reason for lack of power is that many see something of the power of God today but dismiss it, even criticize ministries who are seeking to move in it. If it doesn't have a particular slant or it's too showy, too chaotic, or too anything else, then it is sidelined. It doesn't fit with some predetermined view of how God should do something. Many have a view on how they want to see God's power at work. It must be gentle, or it must be in the context of worship, or through an ordained minister, or in a consecrated building, etc., etc. All these considerations are earthly rather than heavenly. The power of Heaven will never be something that the world values, because it is not designed to advance us in the world. Getting on in the world is not the same as getting on in the Kingdom. Earth is different from Heaven.

To measure the power of God in terms of how far it might work to our benefit on earth, is an attitude that comes from a different Kingdom. The power of God is not for personal success or business gain. It is there to extend and demonstrate the kingdom of Heaven. And the Kingdom, the rule of God, is there to display the power of the God who rules that Kingdom. That is altogether different. You choose God's Kingdom, and God's power will be at work within you, and it will be of real value to the Kingdom. And that will please the Father, for His is the Kingdom, the power, and the glory.

## ENDNOTE

1.  Sid Roth: www.sidroth.org; accessed December 12, 2011.

# CHAPTER 10

# The Glory of Heaven

Father is overwhelmingly zealous for His Kingdom. The creation was built on it; and without His rule and reign, death and destruction will be manifested in it. When Heaven impacts earth, it is the Father's glory that is manifested, because Heaven is full of the glory of God. There is nothing in Heaven that isn't totally impregnated with the glory of God. He fills everything. Glory fills everything. It is all glorious. His plan is that the glory of Heaven is released and manifested on the earth because in the glory realm of His Kingdom, anything becomes possible. Earth cannot forever resist the glory of the kingdom of Heaven.

Churches have tried for too long to do God's work in man's ways and with man's methods and have sacrificed the glory of God in so doing. They have gotten so used to operating without the glory that they no longer really know what it is. They continually ask for God to bless their efforts, their ideas, and their work. But man's ways are earthly, not heavenly.

When we begin to do God's work in God's ways, then we get God's results and the glory of Heaven gets manifested. But none of this will make sense to rational people. The things of the Spirit, the things of Heaven, are foreign to them. The glory of Heaven cannot alight on them. God cannot anoint flesh.

God declares in Haggai 2 that the latter glory will be greater than the former. By the former, I believe that Haggai is referring to Solomon's glory. This was the pinnacle of Israel's history. Solomon's temple was incredible. His wealth, fame, reputation, household, even his cutlery reflected the glory that God had bestowed over him. It was like nothing before or since in history. Solomon's fame spread throughout the known world. Royals from many lands came, including the Queen of Sheba, to see what it was all about. She said:

> *The report I heard in my own country about your achievements and your wisdom is true. But I did not believe these things until I came and saw with my own eyes. Indeed, not even half was told me; in wisdom and wealth you have far exceeded the report I heard. How happy your people must be! How happy your officials, who continually stand before you and hear your wisdom!* (1 Kings 10:6-8)

Yet, what is to come, says Haggai, will be far superior in every measure. The glory of God will totally eclipse the glory of Solomon. Heaven's glory will always overshadow any glory earth has to offer. The challenge is not just to encounter the glory of God, but to carry it.

## THE GLORY OF HEAVEN TOUCHING EARTH

Isaiah's vision in Isaiah 6 was that *his train fills* (and keeps on filling) *the temple.* Imagine it. The picture is of an entourage following a king, which is a symbol of His glory; and it fills and somehow keeps filling the temple. The temple is full, and still it keeps filling and filling. The Father's plan is that this fullness of glory is manifested on the earth. He wants to fill the earth to the full, and keep filling it—fullness on fullness with His glory. In fact, not just Isaiah 6, but think of any scene in Heaven that the Scriptures reveal to us—the Father desires that the glory manifested there is also manifested on earth. It's awesome!

So whenever Heaven touches earth, a measure of the Father's glory is released. The more of Heaven that touches earth, the more of the Father's glory is released. And when that happens and people respond to His glory, supernatural provision occurs. God cannot work where there is no faith response. But where there is, bodies are healed, minds are renewed, oppression is lifted, finances are released, and circumstances come into line with the Kingdom and will of God. This is God's intention—don't allow it to be stolen from you.

There is no lack in Heaven, and so to the degree that Heaven is manifested on earth will be the degree that lack on earth will be lifted. There need be no deficits. Yes, in our natural state we do have lacks and deficits. Romans 3:23 says, "all have sinned and come short of the glory of God." We now live with a glory deficit. Sin has robbed us of the fullness of the glory that God intended we should have. But our sin is already forgiven. Our past sin, our present sin, and even our future sin is already forgiven. Jesus has already died. He has done it all. There is no more to do. There is no need to struggle with it.

Praying more, reading the Word more, serving more, will not make up the glory deficit we have. But whatever you focus on will multiply. Focus on sin, and even if you keep repenting, you'll not see the glory. Focus on the glory, and it will be the glory that will multiply in your life. What you look upon you will become. Let's become less sin conscious and more glory conscious.

But we were never created to have a glory deficit. It doesn't sit with us very well. We instinctively know something is missing. When sin was released into the earth, glory ceased coming out of Heaven. The whole earth suffered and continues to suffer from a glory deficit. Now our role is to stand before God and to release His glory back into the earth. The glory of God is meant to be a "now" inheritance for us. Paul in Romans 8:17 says that if we suffer with Him, we shall also be glorified with Him. I was brought up to believe that the suffering was down here, and the glory was up there—afterward. But the verse doesn't say that. It's here and now that we need Heaven's glory!

And because you're a son or daughter of the Father of glory, you are an heir of everything the Father has, together with Jesus. Everything He has is yours. And He has glory in abundance. Jesus said in John 17:22 as He prayed to His Father, "I have given them [the disciples and us] the glory that You gave Me." We have been given the same glory that the Father gave to Jesus—and it is for the now!

## PRESS IN TO GET PREGNANT

Now we can either leave all this stuff on one side as very interesting but theoretical, or we can hunger to enter in, and hunger to experience what the Scriptures plainly say. Job 22:21 exhorts us to "agree with God." Let's just come into agreement with what God has said in His Word, instead of saying to God, "I hear Your word, but my experience is this." The implication: I'm believing my experience over Your Word, or I'm believing what I've always been taught instead of opening myself to something new from You.

It's not really relevant what your experience or lack of it is.

The gospel, the whole gospel, does exactly what it says! Trouble is, we haven't read everything! There's a lot more good news than we have realized. There's nothing wrong with the Scriptures. It's God's Word. So forget your past experiences. Press in to get more. It's waiting to be discovered. In the natural, you don't get pregnant by merely dating! There has to be a more intimate encounter. So in the spiritual, nothing of His glory will get birthed in your life by just dating God on a Sunday morning. Getting pregnant is what we want, and it requires us to encounter God in His ways, not just in ours. It means meeting Him on His terms, rather than inviting Him to come to our meeting.

I believe we're coming into a season where Father wants us to encounter Him in His ways and not just in our ways. He encounters us in our ways through healing our bodies, supplying our needs, sorting out our relationships, and the like. All this is good and is manifesting the kingdom of Heaven.

However, His ways are something altogether different. It means us going into His world, as well as Him coming into our world. We're familiar with the latter, but not much with the former. God wants to bring us to a place where our focus is on Him and His Heaven, rather than on us and our earth. When that happens, then we shall begin to see the light of Heaven impacting the darkness on earth.

Isaiah 60:1-2 reminds us that there are two things on earth at the same time—thick darkness and the glory of the Lord:

> *Arise, shine, for your light has come, and the glory of the Lord rises* [present tense] *upon you. See, darkness covers the earth and thick darkness is over the peoples, but the Lord rises upon you and His glory appears over you.*

The glory of the Lord is only going to rise on us and appear over us as we get into Heaven's glory and allow it to get all over us. But the majority of Christians know very little of the glory of God. I've spent most of my Christian life without knowing this stuff, but I'm pressing in now according to the Scriptures. Yes, there is thick darkness over the people of God. They are sedated—but the alarm is going off! And the glory of the Lord rises upon you, if you'll allow it.

What is in Heaven, that which is impregnated with His glory, is to be joined and integrated together with what is on earth—you. If you're on earth, you qualify! God wants to manifest His Heaven, His glory over you. The glory that is in Heaven wants to be joined with you, wants to be integrated with you, and wants to impregnate you under the lordship of Jesus. The heavenly glory that Moses experienced at Sinai was clear and obvious. Everyone saw it. But Moses didn't get it from anything on earth. He got it directly from Heaven, from having a serious God encounter.

Father wants to manifest Heaven among us, to us, through us, over us, and in us! That's the deal. That's what Christ died for. It isn't that we might get goose bumps, shake a little in a meeting, fall on the floor, and then go away unchanged. The aim is that we go from glory to glory. The problem is we know nothing about God's glory!

Moses experienced something more than a sense of God's presence; and therefore he experienced more than a sense of God's glory. He said to God, "Show me Your glory," not "Tell me about it" (Exod. 33:18). Moses knew what he wanted. He was hungry for God, and hunger goes a long way with God. Hunger can take you from just a sense of God's glory to experiencing its fullness. Bill Johnson, senior pastor of Bethel Church in Redding, California, says that we seldom find what we're not hungry for.[1] So one of our major issues is that we have become satisfied with what we have, poor though that is. Either we have not been taught that there is more, or we have become so earthly minded that we are of no heavenly use.

Moses was hungry, but was this to be a unique experience for Moses only? Paul, in Second Corinthians, refers to this experience of Moses as a precursor of a New Testament experience that is much greater. Everything we read in the Old Testament is a shadow of what we are able to move in under the New Covenant. But we've never been taught it. We've never expected it. We've been scared of it. We've covered up our lack of glory with seeking excellence. That search has produced an outcome that pleases man, but disappoints God. Man-made order can never substitute for the glory of God.

## KNOWLEDGE OF THE GLORY

The truth is that we can have the fullness of His glory. It is often painfully true that our experience to date doesn't even measure up to the shadow in the Old, let alone the fullness of the New. But we start with what the Word says. Once God drops His revelation into us, then we may begin to experience it for ourselves. But to experience, even to understand something of the glory of the Lord, we need to know what it is. That is why Habakkuk prophesied that "the earth will be filled with the *knowledge* of the glory of the Lord, as the waters cover the sea" (Hab. 2:14). And how do the waters cover the sea? Deep, full and complete, 100 percent. This is what Habakkuk prophesied, and God is calling us to be part of the fulfillment of that prophesy. Knowledge and revelation are important. And the longer we take to understand the glory, the longer it's going to take for this knowledge to cover the earth.

Jesus said that we would know the truth, and the truth—that we know—would set us free. If we don't know about something, we are not going to be able to recognize it or move in it. So revelation is the first prerequisite to experiencing and reflecting Heaven's glory. And, by the way, who else is going to make this knowledge known in all the earth? If we don't, who else is there? This is what God now invites us to partner in with Him.

I believe that this is part of what a new move of God will be about. As Heaven is manifested on earth, my bit of earth, it is the glory of God that is released—and that will attract the world. Isaiah 60:1,3 says, "Arise, shine, your light has come and the glory of the Lord rests upon you. Nations will come to your light." What is this saying? People will be attracted to you when the glory of Heaven rests upon you. Yes, the spirit of glory is supposed to rest on you. First Peter 4:14 says, "You are blessed, for the Spirit of glory and of God rests on you."

The Hebrew word for glory is *cabode*. It means weight or weighty. It is not just the felt presence of God or a sense of God's presence. Rather, it is the active and dynamic, manifested presence of God. It is the fullness of the presence of God. When His glory falls, human flesh dives for the floor. John saw Jesus in His glory in Revelation 1 and fell as dead. In the Old Testament when the glory came, the priests couldn't function. In the New Testament, the glory of God filled the prison where Paul and Silas were and there was an earthquake. Things happen when the glory is allowed to be manifested. And we are privileged to have a measure of God's own glory on us.

But it is God's intention that we move into more glory, from one degree where we are now, to another, and so on, and so on. This glory is meant to make a difference. It isn't there for show. In fact, let's be honest, it hardly shows at all at the moment. We've a long way to go. But this is something we're supposed to live in.

In fact, it is a command over our lives. Second Corinthians 4:6 says, "For God, who said [commanded], "Let light shine out of darkness," made [ordained] His light shine in our hearts to give us the light of the knowledge of God's glory...." God wants to give us more of the knowledge of the glory; and He has commanded, He has ordained His light to shine in your heart to do this. This command is of the same order, it has the same creative power, as that original command in Genesis, "Let there be light," in the beginning. This knowledge is that important. This isn't just a niche theology for the few. This is supposed to be mainstream—and it will be one day. I hope I live to see it.

## MULTIPLICATION OF GLORY

When Jesus speaks to His Father, the conversation is all about the glory. John 17:1 gives us a rare insight into Jesus' relationship with His Father:

> *After Jesus said this, He looked toward heaven and prayed: "Father, the time has come. Glorify Your Son, that Your Son may glorify You."*

The first thing that Jesus wants is for His Father to be glorified in Heaven. This verse then tells us that the only way for the Father to be glorified in Heaven from the earth is if the Father Himself glorifies what is on earth, which will be reflected back to the Father in Heaven. "Glorify Your Son [on earth], that Your Son may glorify You [in Heaven]." It has to start in Heaven, because that's where the glory is. There is only one glory. In all that has been created and even that which has not been created, there is only one glory—and that belongs to the Father. All the glory is His. There is no glory that is not His.

*Yours, LORD, is the greatness and the power and the glory and the majesty and the splendor, for everything in heaven and earth is Yours* (1 Chronicles 29:11).

But Heaven's glory is something given, received, and reflected back to Heaven. The Father gives glory to the Son because He loves Jesus. Jesus gives back glory to the Father by doing what the Father says to do. Remember: Jesus said He did only what the Father says, and by doing what the Father says, the glory is reflected back to the Father, who then pours out more to glorify the Son, who gives the glory to the Father in Heaven, and so on. There's a multiplication of glory. That's how we go from one degree of glory to another.

But not only does Jesus receive the Father's glory because He did only what He saw the Father doing, Jesus also receives the Father's glory because of us. We might well ask, why? For we know our own hearts. It's amazing, "All I have is Yours, and all You have is Mine. And glory has come to Me through them" (John 17:10). Glory accrues to Jesus even through us. Now how does that happen? "For I gave them the words You gave Me and they accepted them. They knew with certainty that I came from You, and they believed that You sent Me" (John 17:8).

Jesus gets glory as we declare who He is and what He has said. And when we declare who He is and what He's said, we get another measure of His glory in return. The reverse is also true. We steal the glory due to Jesus when we do not declare who He is, and when we neglect to say the words He said, but rather say things from ourselves that we have not heard from the Father.

The Father's glory comes to us only in His presence.

*I* [Jesus] *have brought You* [the Father] *glory on earth by completing the work You gave Me to do. And now, Father, glorify Me in Your presence with the glory I had with You before the world began* (John 17:4-5).

Take His presence away, and His glory goes away. It's like a torch in a mirror. Take the torch away and the reflection also goes away. It is His presence that brings the glory. That's why encountering God is so important. Not just getting a sense of His presence, but pushing through to experience His active and dynamic presence. If we're not encountering His presence, we're not in a position to receive more of His glory on our lives. And, by the way, He doesn't always do it to fit in with our human time schedules. That's not how the kingdom of Heaven works.

Jesus hosted God's presence all the time, and so God's glory was manifested in His life all the time. Once He came out of the desert in the power of the Spirit, His face was not veiled. He didn't hide the glory that was on Him. It was obvious that this was not just another rabbi. The glory of God on Jesus was there, and it manifested in the authority He had, the revelation He had, the grace, the forgiveness, the miraculous. After His first miracle, it says in John 2:11, "He thus revealed His glory, and His disciples put their faith in Him."

So the face of Jesus was and is unveiled. But what about our faces? We also are supposed to have unveiled faces, unblocked faces, reflecting the glory He has given us.

Yes, we have been given the same glory that He had. And yes, it is meant to manifest in the same ways that it manifested in Him—it's called fruit. John 15:8 says, "This is to My Father's glory, that you bear much fruit, showing yourselves to be My disciples." Don't just think about the fruit of the Spirit when you hear the word fruit. What Jesus means here, is doing what He did and saying what He said. How did the people in Acts know that Peter, John, and the others were disciples of Jesus? They did the same things He did, in the same way He did them! The manifestation of Jesus' glory was all over them. In fact, they began to do the *even greater works*—Peter's shadow, Paul's prayer cloths, and so on.

There should be no veils, no blockages, and no hindrances in either receiving the glory or reflecting it. In fact, it is only when our faces are unveiled, unblocked, can we either receive or reflect it back. Only then can we see Him face to face, because it is *in the face of Jesus Christ* that the knowledge of the glory of God exists. Glory is supposed to be our covering. But just as our first ancestors, Adam and

Eve, we content ourselves with a false covering. We just do not want to dispense with the fig leaves.

But if we are to be transformed, that's what has to happen. It is the intrinsic nature of the glory, that when we are exposed to it in our intimate encounter face to face, we are progressively transformed into His likeness. It's just what the glory does. Second Corinthians 3:18 says:

> *And we, who with unveiled faces all reflect the Lord's glory, are being transformed into His likeness with ever-increasing glory* [or from one degree to another], *which comes from the Lord, who is the Spirit.*

This is what the Spirit is here to do with us, because that is what He did with Jesus. And as He does it with us, it will bring glory to Jesus. John 16:14 says, "He [the Spirit] will glorify Me because it is from Me that He will receive what He will make known to you." So, even as the Spirit is bringing you revelation now about this, glory is being brought to Jesus.

The biggest thing Heaven wants to do is to impact earth with the glory of God; and the way that God has prescribed that it is going to be done, is through you. No other way. In Second Corinthians 4:7, Paul calls this glory a divine treasure that we carry around in our jars of clay—our bodies. And although these bodies are weak, sinful, and subject to troubles of every kind, he calls them light and momentary compared with the eternal weight of glory we carry. We carry an eternal weight of glory now!

Jesus displayed the amazing glory of the Father as He walked the earth. Michele Perry of Iris Ministries identifies some of these instances in her blog:

> Jesus walking through walls (Jn 20:19 how else did He get in the room with the door shut?), glowing (Lk 11), turning invisible (Lk 4:30, again how else did He just walk right through an angry mob bent on killing Him?), hearing peoples thoughts (Lk 5:22, 6:8, 11:17), changing weather patterns (Mt 8:26, Mk 4:39, Lk

8:24), miracles of altering one substance into another (Jn 2), walking on water (Jn 6:19), translocating (Lk 24:31, Lk 24:35, Jn 6:21), flying (or ascending if you prefer, Lk 24:51) to just name a few!

The lesser read pages of church history are filled with radical lovers of Jesus walking in similar phenomena as their normal. No one batted an eye when St Francis floated to the treeline in worship. These things so often relegated to the occult only belong to darkness because we have given them over to it. For every counterfeit, there is a true. It is time we step deeper into our inheritance in Jesus than ever before. Not out of some crazy lust for power, but out of an overflow of being so in love with Him we become possessed with His fullness.

I really believe Papa wants to pour this level of glory out on the earth and MORE, the greater things than these. I know it is coming and I am diving lower and closer to His burning heart to embrace an Enoch walk, however He chooses His glory to be revealed through this daughter of His.[2]

These are some of the greater things that Jesus declared we would walk in. It's what we were created for.

But a note of caution: glory has been given to us by the Father, but its manifestation in us is in our control. We can allow it to invade us, we can make a way for it and allow it to be reflected back to the Father—or we can allow it to dissipate. Hosea 4:7 says, "The more the priests increased, the more they sinned against Me; they exchanged their Glory, for something disgraceful" (NIV 1984). The priest had a glory, but they dissipated it. Religion has a way of bringing everything of God down to a human level, and once under man's control, there is no more room for God's supernatural glory.

But there's a promise. Jesus' promise to us is that we *will* see His glory, we *will* see the fullness of the glory He had with the Father before creation.

> *Father, I want those You have given Me, to be with Me where I am, and to see My glory, the glory You have given Me because You loved Me before the creation of the world* (John 17:24).

And if you know Jesus at all, you know this won't be a self-admiration session. It will rather be: "All this glory that My Father has given Me," says Jesus, "is yours!" And, what's more, it begins now. It isn't for the sweet by and by! You're already a citizen of Heaven. You are seated at the right hand of the Father *now*. This heavenly glory is yours to live in, to move in—to fulfill your destiny.

## ENDNOTES

1. From a weekly sermon by Bill Johnson: http://www.bjm. org.

2. Michele Perry: Iris Ministries. http://irisminsudan.org; accessed December 12, 2011.

# Contact the Author

If you would like Geoff and the Your Kingdom Come team
to visit your town, church, or organization,
please email:
geoff@yourkingdomcome.org.uk

We would be delighted to serve you in any way possible.

# Another exciting title from
# EVANGELISTA MEDIA™

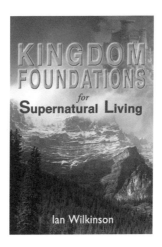

## KINGDOM FOUNDATIONS FOR SUPERNATURAL LIVING
### by Ian Wilkinson

Having a solid Kingdom foundation and learning to grow up spiritually prepare you to properly do the works of Jesus in the will of God. *Kingdom Foundations for Supernatural Living* teaches you how to mature into an authentic Spirit-empowered and Spirit-controlled son or daughter of God capable of doing the things Jesus did without being unauthorized or lawless.

Some want shortcuts into the supernatural life, but a strong scriptural foundation must be in place as the launching point into the genuine life in the Spirit that God wants you to experience. This foundations also provides a basis for discerning and validating all teachings and preachings you hear. All of creation is eagerly waiting for mature sons and daughters of God to reveal the supernatural life. The world is waiting for you!

ISBN: 978-88-96727-49-2

ORDER NOW FROM EVANGELISTA MEDIA™
Tel: +39 085 4716623 • Fax: +39 085 9090113
Email: orders@evangelistamedia.com
www.evangelistamedia.com

Additional copies of this book and other book
titles from EVANGELISTA MEDIA™
and DESTINY IMAGE™ EUROPE
are available at your local bookstore.

We are adding new titles every month!

To view our complete catalog online, visit us at:
**www.evangelistamedia.com**

Send a request for a catalog to:

**Via della Scafa, 29/14
65013 Città Sant'Angelo (Pe), ITALY
Tel. +39 085 4716623 • Fax +39 085 9090113
info@evangelistamedia.com**

*"Changing the World, One Book at a Time"*

---

Are you an author?

Do you have a "today" God-given message?

## CONTACT US

We will be happy to review your manuscript
for the possibility of publication:

publisher@evangelistamedia.com
http://www.evangelistamedia.com/pages/AuthorsAppForm.htm